Thirty Essays
on the
Gospel of Thomas

COVER:

Photograph 'New Light' taken by the author in Kenwood, North London.

Calligraphy by John Blamires.

BY THE SAME AUTHOR:

The Gospel of Thomas

Newly presented to bring out the
meaning, with Introductions,
Paraphrases and Notes

Thirty Essays on the Gospel of Thomas

by

Hugh McGregor Ross

ELEMENT BOOKS

Copyright © Hugh McGregor Ross 1990

First published in Great Britain in 1990 by
Element Books Limited
Longmead, Shaftsbury, Dorset

Calligraphy for cover and title-page by John Blamires, Brighouse

Cover printed by DDS Colour Printers, Weston-super-Mare

Typeset automatically by Alpha Studio, Stroud, on Linotronic
system linked to author's Amstrad+Topcopy word processor,
all computer controlled. Plantin font 11 point on 13 or 14.5

Special Greek and Coptic words by Linotype Limited, Cheltenham

Printed and bound by Billing and Sons, Worcester

British Library Cataloguing in Publication Data
Ross, Hugh McGregor
Thirty Essays on the Gospel of Thomas
1. Bible. N. T. Apocryphal Gospels. Critical Studies
I. Title
229.8

ISBN 1-85230-183-X

Contents

Acknowledgements

Grateful acknowledgement is made for the quotation of extended passages from the following works: *Advices and Queries*, published 1964 by London Yearly Meeting of the Religious Society of Friends; Trevor Ling, *A History of Religion East and West*, 1968, MacMillan; James M Robinson, *The Nag Hammadi Library in English*, 1977, Brill, Leyden; Maurice Nicoll, *The Mark*, 1954, Robinson and Watkins; Ronald Blackburn, *Salvation in the New Testament Experience*,1989, Friends Quarterly.

Numerous short quotations are acknowledged in footnotes as they occur; those from the Bible are from the Revised Standard Version.

The essay *A Heretical Gospel* made use throughout of Joan O'Grady's book *Heresy*, 1985, Element Books.

Many of the essays have derived great benefit from the two books by members of the Association Métanoïa, Marsanne–26200 Montélimar, France: Phillipe de Suarez, *L'Évangile Selon Thomas*, 1975 version; Émile Gillabert, Pierre Bourgeois, Yves Haas, *Évangile Selon Thomas*, 1979 version.

Preface

The author qualified as an engineer at Cambridge University under Professor Ingles, one of the great teaching engineers of the century. In his inspiring lectures he emphasized the social implications of engineering, and the value of being trained to be adaptable without too much specialization.

Hugh Ross worked initially in research laboratories and then entered the computer industry in its earliest days. At that time the most authoritative view was that there was need for only a few digital computers in Britain. There were a total of only about 40 persons working on them in this country, and he joined a specialist computer company in the week of the very first commercial sale of a computer anywhere in the world (previous ones had been university or military projects). So in his working life he has seen this amazing transition, to the stage where almost every schoolchild has used a computer, many own one, and they can be bought in the high street along with newspapers and sweets.

This 'information technology' revolution that has burst upon us—to which the author made many contributions—has come about by the application of scientific method. Strangely, certain vital features of this are applicable to this book. It relies, first, on keeping one's eyes open, to find some clue; whether it is true or false, correct or in error, does not matter at this stage. Then that clue is followed up, exploring every avenue, until it is either dismissed or found to have value, when it can be built up into a hypothesis or 'scenario' encompassing much else besides.

Applying this to the subject matter of this book, the initial clue was the introduction to the author—we would ordinarily call it by chance—of the first English translation of the Gospel of Thomas, and his noticing that it claims to be the words of the living Jesus; what is more, that it was written down by a disciple who walked about with Jesus and listened to him. This fell on fertile ground, because the author at that time had learnt by family upbringing and through other literary research work that his Quaker approach to Christianity was strongly dependent on the example of Jesus and the nature of his teaching.

Finding that translation difficult, and apparently in some places coloured by copying phrases from the Gospels of the Bible, he set about finding a greater understanding of this Gospel. This necessitated learning the ancient Coptic language of the manuscript. The outcome of that work, spread over nine years, was the *Presentation of the Gospel of Thomas*★ to which this book is a companion.

However, the application of this scientific approach—which perhaps may not come so easily to others whose backgrounds are from theological or literary fields—appears in many other instances in this present volume. Virtually every one of these essays has started from spotting some clue, either in the Gospel of Thomas itself or in religious and spiritual life as the author has experienced it. Each essay has grown out of one of these clues, as a plant grows out of a seed. It is a product of thought and reflection. Apart from a few instances, it is not made up of a collection and synthesis of the writings of others, except insofar as these have contributed to the author's own knowledge and experience. Thus the author does not work in a study lined with books—he chiefly uses the excellent services

★ *The Gospel of Thomas, Newly presented to bring out the meaning, with Introductions, Paraphrases and Notes*, Hugh McGregor Ross, 1987, Sessions of York and Element Books Ltd, Shaftsbury.

of the lending library in his village, linked to the national libraries. Instead, his awareness has more often come during times of meditation, and while walking in the glorious countryside of Gloucestershire or scrambling in the mountains.

The essays have been written over a period of about three years. One of them took a mere hour and forty minutes; another required several months of study involving days spent at the Bodleian Library in Oxford, one of the greatest and most inspiring to work in. They were certainly not written in the sequence they appear in the book. They were done when the author's inner state was at different levels. Accordingly, there is a variableness in them which is both inevitable and intentional. People differ in what they may find of interest or value, and differ from one period of life to another. A beach in which the pebbles are of varied size and colour may be the most delightful.

As each of the hypotheses is presented in an essay its verification does not depend on intensive knowledge. The ordinary reader can do it: all it needs is an open mind; good common-sense; and a willingness to let the words of Jesus— or whoever the Master was—quoted in this Gospel to reach into the depths of one's heart and there to act as a ferment, like the yeast in the dough.

Each of the essays in this book is independent, that it to say it may be read on its own. One of the consequences is that some repetition may be found. In particular, some of the logia are referred to several times, but this is only to be expected as they are capable of being looked at from different points of view. However, the essays are arranged in a kind of sequence, starting with the simplest—dealing with matter of fact topics— and gradually progressing to the more complex and profound themes.

With an approach like this, such essays become a kind of exploration, both for the writer and also for the reader. Some of them in the end may turn out to be following blind alleys, or going off in wrong directions. That matters little. There is nothing authoritative about them. They invite the reader to join the exploration. Some surprises are certain to be in store. Some challenges may arise, some unacceptable. Whatever the outcome, it is hoped that they will be of interest and, being related however indirectly to the words of Jesus, may be of value.

The manuscript of the Gospel of Thomas

To set the scene. The Gospel of Thomas has come down to us from antiquity amongst a group of twelve volumes discovered in 1945 at a site in Egypt mid-way along the Nile. They were buried by the monks of a monastery at a time of persecution, near the present-day town of Nag Hammâdi. This Gospel is of one of 52 books, now known as the Nag Hammâdi Library, which reveal teachings and beliefs of early Christian Churches. It has the introductory statement –

These are the hidden logia

which the living Jesus spoke

and Didymos Judas Thomas wrote.

A logion is a saying, given by a Master, that has both an outer and a deep inner meaning; on finding this, there is great reward for one's life.

The manuscript we have which is the only complete one known of the Gospel of Thomas, is written very clearly in black ink, probably with a quill on papyrus. This was made—and still is for craft work—by cutting long strips of the pith of a reed that grows in Egypt, laying these strips side by side, placing other strips at right angles, then hammering and polishing them. A residual adhesive in the pith makes all the strips stick together, and a practical and durable writing material is obtained. It has a pale golden colour.

A number of tall papyrus sheets were pasted together side by side, then cut and stacked to form a book; a spine was laid at the centre and secured by thongs through two slots into a leather cover, made of antelope skin. The cover has flaps around all the edges, the whole being secured by a tie, to give protection to the contents. The group of folded sheets is correctly named a quire, and the whole a codex. At the time it was a considerable technical achievement to make papyrus sheets of this size, and the whole is enhanced by quite complex tooled patterns on the front cover.

The writing is on both sides of the sheets, each page being correctly termed a folio. It is very clear and easy to read. The Gospel of Thomas occupies twenty folios, and is properly called a book, in the sense of that name being used for each of the Gospels of the Bible. So a number of books are contained in the codex. It was written before it was the practice to use spaces between words, nor is there any punctuation. The scribe filled out each line until there was no more room, without attempting to end the line at the end of a word. Very few people then would have been able to read, so it was probably primarily used for reading out aloud, there being some marks to aid pronunciation and emphasis. An important detail is that the last line is filled out with little marks, which shows that the monk who wrote it copied everything from the version he was working from. The title comes at the finish.

Some of the sheets are damaged at the corners, and there are small gaps within some pages. Of course after sixteen or more hundred years the papyrus is brittle and, as we shall see in the next essay, the codices had a hazardous time after they were found until they have finished up secured between sheets of clear plastic in the Coptic Museum in Cairo. Also the scribe made some mistakes, typically where repeated letters are omitted, such as we might make in copying 'titivated' as 'tivated'. However these are matters that scholars can resolve, and it is fortunate that none of these defects in the text have any significance for the meaning.

Like all the books of the Nag Hammâdi Library, our manuscript of the Gospel of Thomas is written predominantly in Coptic. This was a synthetic or manufactured language, in contrast to English which has grown up over many centuries assimilating contributions from many sources. The Egyptian spoken language was first written in hieroglyphs. This picture representation gradually became inconvenient or inadequate, and was replaced by an alphabetic form of writing, Demotic. By the last centuries B.C. and the first A.D., philosophical, religious and spiritual writings were coming into Egypt written in Greek. It was found that Demotic did not have the vocabulary to permit these to be translated. Also Greek was very widely used in trade and commerce. So Coptic was invented, specifically to aid understanding and simplify translation. Of course, it was a gradual process during the first and second centuries, with later development. Coptic is written with Greek capital letters, together with six from Demotic; it was fortunate for the present author that he came to his studies on this Gospel after having done pioneering work on putting Greek letters into computers. Coptic takes various forms, with rather different vocabularies and grammar; the Gospel of Thomas is written in Sahidic, the commonest, from the northern Nile area.

Coptic is now practically confined to the liturgy of the Coptic Christian Church in Egypt and Ethiopia. It is very difficult to find an expert in its use. Fortunately Dr W E Crum gave his working life at Oxford University to a study of it so that his Coptic dictionary, giving equivalents in English and Greek, is available—and is used as the first stage in translations into any modern language. Other books have such restricted sales that some are merely photo-reproduced from manuscript or typescript.*

★ For details see the References at the end of the *Presentation* .

It is generally considered that the Gospel of Thomas, in the complete form we have it, was first written in Greek. It is not known when the translation into Coptic was made. The manuscript we have is no doubt a later copy of that translation. When a list is made of all the different words in the text, about 60 percent are in Coptic (and these are used most frequently) but the remaining 40 percent are left in Greek. This is not unusual to some extent in ancient Coptic texts. However, it is the simple words like man, house, bird, sky, tree that are in Coptic, and those with more sophisticated meanings like gospel, disciple, angel, knowledge, understanding, mystery that are in Greek, although Coptic developed words for these later. Its spelling and use of grammatical constructs is somewhat irregular. All this may indicate that this was an early translation. Further, there are two important Greek words used, metanioa and manochos, that do not have equivalents in other European languages.

The structure of the text is essentially Semitic. That is to say, short phrases are used, which may either build up into a climax or may give contrasting pairs of ideas. This is very different from the Greek form of speech or writing, which we have inherited, of constructing long sentences, with subsidiary clauses, developing a concept and expanding on its features. This structure was first identified by the French workers of the Association Métanoïa, and has been copied into the *Presentation.**

It was not surprising that the phrases were so similar in French and English, it was much more interesting that they also exist in the Coptic, and have been carried through from the original Greek. At least, it indicates the Greek was a record of words spoken in a Semitic idiom.

---

* See the references in the Acknowledgements. These works use an erudite and elegant form of French but, regrettably, are very difficult to obtain.

It is also noteworthy that words are used in the text very precisely. One way in which this shows up is with words that may have synonyms; when the right choice is made a more significant meaning is found in the phrase. To illustrate this three examples may be given: first, in the introductory logion the Coptic word for hidden is the same as that used for the treasure hidden in the field (*logion 109*), not 'secret' or 'obscure' as used in other translations; second, in logion 13 it is three logia that are revealed to Thomas, not 'words' or 'things'; third, the three very particular uses of different Coptic words related to 'to know' discussed in Note 6 to logion 3 in the *Presentation*. Another way the precision shows up is as in two phrases of logion 3 –

>   . . . then you are in poverty,
>   and you are the poverty.

the 'in' and the 'the' are necessary for the full significance. This right and precise use of words, which also takes other forms and permeates the whole, is a distinctive feature of this Gospel and is both a source and a result of awareness of its meanings.

One consequence of this kind of precision is that words, even those used in translation, need to be understood in their intended sense. It is to help with this, and to avoid the even greater mistake of associating meanings that are not intended, that the Notes in the *Presentation* have been offered.

Several passages by early Church writers that have been long known can now be identified as quotations from the Gospel of Thomas, or at least from an equivalent tradition. In addition, portions of the Gospel were discovered at the turn of this century at Oxyrhyncus, the site of another ancient monastery not far to the north along the Nile. They are written in Greek, and are thought to be dated about 200 A.D. These relate to only 18 of the 115 logia, and are extremely fragmentary; it is now possible to fill out the broken places. Comparisons show, in the first place, that the translation into Coptic was done skilfully; secondly, the only differences of any substance is that 'Kingdom' is expanded to 'Kingdom of God', and in logion 5 a phrase is added at the end that has been reconstructed as –

'. . . and buried that [will] not [be raised up (?)]'
which, it is suggested, is a reference to resurrection. The opinions of experts seem to be divided whether both these represent additions to that version or deletions from ours.

At the time of writing a quite substantial bibliography about the Gospel of Thomas has grown up. There may be perhaps twenty books, in whole or part, and getting on for one hundred articles in journals.* Most of these are by and for scholars or experts in theological fields, and it is legitimate to say that a gradually increasing recognition of its value is developing. The books by the French workers of the Association Métanoïa are distinguished by having an interest in, a deep awareness of, and a willingness to present the inner meanings of the logia.

★ A bibliography of the complete Nag Hammâdi Library is maintained in David M Scholer, *Nag Hammadi Bibliography 1948–1969*, *Brill, 1971; plus* Bibliographia Gnostica: Supplementum I–XI, 1971–1983; it being said 'The Supplements are to be integrated and republished as *Nag Hammadi Bibliography 1970 –1983, Brill.*'

Adventures of the
Gospel of Thomas

Like every good story by Agatha Christie that starts off with
a murder, so do the adventures of the manuscript we have of
the Gospel of Thomas. Not just one murder, but multiple
murders. And not just once, but on two occasions.

These murders in fact occurred previous to key events for
the manuscript, but they have a direct bearing on events. Let
us initially consider the first occasion. In the early-300s A.D.
Diocletian was unifying the rule of the Roman empire and
enhancing the status of the emperor. This required giving to
him homage and sacrifices, which Christians and Jews could
not do. Seeing the Christians as a potential threat to himself
and the Roman religion, persecution resulted. Also at that
time considerable momentum had been built up by those
sections of the Christian Church who considered themselves to
be paramount and were consolidating their doctrines and
liturgy. As orthodoxy became established, anything different
was termed heretical and to be condemned. A characteristic
of many Christian Churches, which distinguishes them from
almost all other religions, is that they persecute each other,
especially any deemed heretical. ·

There were then Christian Churches in north Africa whose
beliefs and practices were different from those of the main-
stream Churches. So in the early years of that century
persecution broke out against them, buildings and sacred
objects were desecrated, all books destroyed, the leaders killed
or exiled, and the people scattered. Sometimes soldiery was

used, sometimes priests stirred up the mob. Such persecution is to obliterate concepts and beliefs, which are spread from person to person especially within families. The technique was well spelled out centuries later by Machiavelli. We now think of him as devilish, but really he was a highly proficient civil servant. In *The Prince* he advises his ruling master that to deal with a rival his brothers and sisters, children, nephews and nieces should all be disposed of, if necessary by murder.

Partly as a consequence, members of such Churches moved away into the desert forming at first communities round some teacher, each person living in a simple hut or cell. Soon however these groups became more organized and, especially under St Pachomius many monasteries were set up in Egypt, each collected within a stout defensive wall. It is thought there were 50,000 such monks there.

It was in 367 that Archbishop Athanasius of Alexandria sent out an edict to establish the canonical books of the New Testament, and to condemn all heretical teachings and apocryphal books. This came after a period of persecutions over doctrinal matters, during which he had himself been exiled five times, despite being greatly respected by his followers. He was undoubtedly seeking to unify the Christian faith, and perhaps he was taking the practical view that it was important to save the lives of his people and avoid any repetition of the bloodshed of previous decades.

The monks at the monastery of St Palamon at Chenoboskia about 600 kilometres up the Nile would have had experience or at least memories of persecutions of anything branded heretical. So, on this edict reaching them 'as a rule to live by' it is surmised that some of the monks took certain bound volumes of their library, put them in a tall jar and sealed the lid with bitumen, and buried it in the sand beside a large rock near the foot of the escarpment that rises from the fertile river valley to the desert beyond. We know that this must have been an act to preserve them, for the practice then was to dispose of anything by fire or by letting the river sweep it away, like the baby Moses. Therefore these volumes must have been regarded as treasures, to be saved from calamity, and the act can be looked on as a final homage to the records of the teachings and faith they lived by.

Thus the volume containing the Gospel of Thomas, along with eleven or twelve other volumes, lay snug in the earthenware jar, embraced by the warm dry sand and shielded 'where no moth comes near to devour, and no worm destroys'. In that state it escaped the eventual destruction of their monastery, the invading army of the Persians in the seventh century, and the complete Arab conquest that began soon after and lasted for eight hundred years only to be followed by Turkish dominion.

It also escaped the consequences of the subsequent confirmations of the canonical books of the Christian Church. The Gospel of Thomas is specifically mentioned in the list of books that are banned and are to be destroyed—real glowing terms are used 'to be damned in the inextricable shackles of anathema for ever'. That condemnation was certainly effective, because no other complete copy of this Gospel has survived.

Unlike so many other documents of the early Church that have come down to us, it escaped the attentions of redactors. Whereas the Hebrew scriptures might not be changed in the slightest degree, those who copied the Christian gospels—while taking great care to avoid mistakes—felt a certain freedom to make revisions to align one with another or to incorporate the latest understandings. One only has to compare modern translations of the New Testament to see this in progress. In itself this might not matter much; the trouble arose because of the tendency to throw away each earlier version, either because worn out or considered to be superseded.

Our copy of the Gospel of Thomas escaped being discovered

in the sixteenth century. Then Tyndale was put on the bonfire for translating the Bible into English—the Gospel of Thomas would most certainly have gone on too. If it had been discovered in any of the centuries of the Inquisition, it would quickly have been engulfed. By the nineteenth century it could not have survived the kind of outcry that befell Darwin, who after all only tilted at the Old Testament. For us, it must be regarded as a miraculous escape that it remained hidden in that jar until the power of the Church over temporal matters is so weakened as to permit it to survive.

Now for the second twist from Agatha Christie. Near the ruined monastery of St Palamon beyond the present-day town of Nag Hammâdi, nearly 600 kilometres from Cairo, the Nile takes a sweep, leaving an area of land about 15 kilometres long by 8 at its widest. In the middle of our century the rule of the central authorities largely by-passed this district, order being maintained by the strongest local family. However, it was an order in which time-honoured blood feuds were maintained. One of the villagers, father of a family, was employed to guard irrigation works and, suspecting an intruder in the dark to be a thief, killed him. Next night he too was murdered, and the head of his victim laid beside his body.

About six months later, his two sons with other neighbours went out with their camels to dig near the foot of the escarpment for a fertile soil used on their fields. In digging, one of them came upon a jar. There was discussion whether it might contain a jinn or have some other sinister effect but, greatly daring, the elder son broke open the sealing. Out came what has been called a glittering cloud, no doubt particles from the contents, and looking inside were a number of old-looking volumes. In fairness, he thought it right to share these out amongst the whole party, seven of them, either as whole books or by splitting them up. However, the others would not take them, so he bundled them together and brought them back to the family home.

Suspicion for the murder of the father fell on a young man who, about a month after the discovery of the jar, was espied asleep beside the road nearby. The mother had urged her sons to keep their mattocks sharp, and saw the chance to avenge her loss. So her sons went out and hacked the young man to pieces. Although it may be macabre to say it, and whatever our feelings may be about these events, they make it possible to identify the date of the discovery of our manuscript of the Gospel of Thomas quite accurately as December 1945. And, in fact, all this was only a prelude, for the feud ricocheted over several years and many more corpses, creating a fear that made it extremely difficult to persuade the finders to reveal to later inquirers the exact details of their discovery.

As for the books brought home and dumped in the straw beside the cooking oven, the mother, distraught from the loss of her husband, saw these only as an evil omen, and some of the loose pages and covers went into the fire. But the sons had visions of riches in these finds and retrieved them. Yet it was important to get them out of the way, lest they either be used as evidence by police investigating (unsuccessfully, it turned out) the murders, or in case they should be seized by the authorities—for everyone knew that only paltry compensation would be paid compared with the price on the black market.

In this atmosphere of ignorance, fear and suspicion attempts were made to sell the volumes amongst some of the neighbours in the village, asking first an Egyptian pound for one with a promise of there being others, this being reduced to a few piasters (100 to E£) or cigarettes. But there were no takers. Some were left with a camel driver, but sent back as worthless. In time they were identified as being written in Coptic, presumably because it was not Arabic, but the local priest of the Coptic Church turned down an offer for E£3. Another Coptic priest regarded them as interesting and housed a few volumes for some time, until they were seen by his son, a teacher, on a visit. The son borrowed one, but at his home was told to take it away as police were making their investigations. However, a few days later he was offered a second, for which there was some paltry barter.

It seems the volumes did get placed with various persons in the village, one of whom was notorious as a one-eyed outlaw. Perhaps his contempt for authority overcame his fear. He made contact with a travelling dealer in antiquities, and together with a jeweller friend the three men took two volumes to Cairo, one of these containing (although it was not known at the time) the Gospel of Thomas. At an antiquities shop there the offering price to a member of a French archeological institute in Cairo was E£700, but that fell through, although later the outlaw did sell them to the travelling dealer for E£200 each, enabling him to improve his position and buy farm land. A few other volumes were rounded up from the villagers, one being bought for E£12 plus 40 oranges and some being bartered for sugar and tea, and sold on. Other volumes, which do not directly concern us, had more spectacular adventures involving threats to life, until they all reached dealers in Cairo, at price tags of about E£300 each.

At this stage westerners became involved, with asking prices multiplied ten or fifteen times. However, the only identification of the contents of the documents that by then had been made was that they were gnostic papers. Then, this was sufficient to quench the interest of established libraries, who were not willing to take up the offers. Added to that, it is clear from the detailed reports that it was a delicate matter to try to sell goods, the nature or interest of which were not known by anybody, at a sufficiently high price to enable the seller to feel, ultimately, that he had not lost a great opportunity. And also to do so in a sufficiently clandestine manner that the transactions were not brought to the notice of the authorities, whereupon all chance of fortunes would be lost.

Amongst the various moves, most of the volumes were put into the nominal ownership of an individual who, being not a dealer, would be exempt from taxes. They were offered to the Cairo Coptic Museum, but at too high a price to be acceptable. Next, the authorities amended the law to make discovered manuscripts, like artifacts, national property. However, this sequestration was challenged by the lady who 'owned' them, a legal complication that extended over several years and came to nought. Through all this period the volumes were contained merely in an old locked valise at the Service des Antiquities in Cairo.

However, by 1956 the owner was indemnified and the first photographs of the manuscripts began to be shared out amongst scholars. This however became associated with most deeply held views about the rights to publish them. It has to be borne in mind that much of the work done on ancient sources of Christianity takes the form of making comparisons and extracting significance from small quotations, even of individual words. To have a complete document that is new offers an opportunity to establish a reputation in being the first to publish from it. Fortunately, however, the Gospel of Thomas did not suffer such serious delays as others of the books. At the outbreak of the Suez Crisis Professor Gilles Quispel who had been working on the texts in Cairo had escaped to Europe with photographic copies, from which a team of four experts re-established the Coptic text from its very early form and translated it into English, this being published in 1959.*

In the end UNESCO was brought in to create order out of this situation. A particular objective was to make photographs

---

* A Guillaumont, H-Ch Puech, G Quispel, W Till and Yassah 'Abd Al Masîh, *The Gospel according to Thomas*, 1959, Brill, Leiden.

available.   Some had been taken in 1952, and more in 1957, but these were not good enough for the full sized high quality versions (facsimiles) that were intended.   Ultimately an adequate set was taken in 1962, but with the intervention of the war between Egypt and Israel and all the problems of joint working between Cairo, editors in America and the publisher in Holland, it was not until 1978 that the complete set of facsimiles was published.*   These, which may be seen in the major libraries, show the extreme quality of the manuscripts, and our amazing good fortune that they have survived their great variety of adventures—each and every one of which, if it had turned out the other way, would have resulted in their destruction.

* B Layton and others, *The Facsimile Edition of the Nag Hammâdi Codices*, Brill, 1974 to 1978.   With an *Introduction* volume.   Complemented by a series of volumes on each of the Codices, published up to 1989.   The Gospel of Thomas is in Codex II, folios 32–51;   on page 4 is another photograph showing the whole book opened at folios 50 and 51.   (Unfortunately, the photographs of the last page of the Gospel of Thomas are poor.)

Also J M Robinson, *The Discovery of the Nag Hammadi Codices*, The Biblical Archaeologist, vol 42, No 4, Autumn 1979.

Dating the Gospel of Thomas

The Gospel of Thomas claims to be a set of sayings of the living Jesus written down by the Apostle Thomas. Here we are not concerned with the validity of the claim (merely allowing the possibility that it may be valid) nor with the content or meanings of the Gospel, but only with its dating.

Let us travel backwards in time, giving attention to each of the milestones available to us. In 1945 the complete manuscript of the Gospel was dug up from the sands of Egypt, amongst a collection of books. From a study of the handwriting and especially the bindings, some of the others of which were stiffened by re-used papyrus documents of accounts and so on, these books are usually dated to the first half of the fourth century.

The situation in which the books came to be buried related to the gradual establishment of orthodoxy amongst the previous differing Christian Churches, and the most probable occasion is considered to have been the proclamation of an acceptable group of scriptures by Archbishop Athanasius of the Alexandrian Church in 367 A.D. The manuscript we have is a copy, and it is not possible to date when it was made, except to note that it could have been a substantial time before the set of books were completed and buried.

It is known that Archbishop Hippolatus of Lyon (France) who died about 325 A.D. condemned the Gospel of Thomas as heretical. Therefore copies of it must have been circulating rather widely by that time, sufficiently so to make it worth banning.

The master version, from which the manuscript was copied, was translated into Coptic from Greek, and the somewhat primitive nature of the Coptic suggests a date perhaps in the third century. A Greek version of the Gospel, although very fragmentary, is regarded as being from about the year 200 A.D.

A number of quotations from the Gospel of Thomas exist in the writings of early Churchmen spanning across the first four centuries. ★   Until the Nag Hammâdi find there was little more known about its contents.

The date that is given by most scholars for the composition of the whole Gospel in substantially the form we have it is 140 A.D.   It is also considered that this composition took place at Edessa in Mesopotamia.   This takes into consideration the use of it for quotations in writings later than that date, and also the inclusion in it of concepts and words that were distinctive to a Church in that place and time.   (See essay *Coloration*)

Consideration now has to be given to the form in which it became available for that composition.   On the one hand, people's memories were then more acute than ours, because our availability of printed records makes it less important to remember precisely.   It is just possible that the sayings, the phrases and even words have been passed down for three generations, as oral traditions.   On the other hand, it is considered to be just as probable that the sayings existed in a written document that was taken over by the final editor or redactor.   There is no firm evidence to show whether or not that text may have been the same or different from the final version;   the probability is that some sayings were the same, and others were changed.

However, the view is held that the final version was not just an invention, or even a variant of sayings that were already

★   A selection with some quotations are given in E Hennecke, *New Testament Apocrypha*, vol. 1, 1963, Lutterworth, pages 278–282. See also in *Évangile Selon Thomas*, 1979 version, Éditions Métanïoa, pages 127–152.

available from what has become the Gospels of the Bible. There are overlaps, but not sufficient to account for the whole. Therefore consideration may be given to how the earlier, or prototype, version of the sayings were made.

One possibility that cannot be ruled out is that the sayings were received, to start the oral tradition or a written version, by the Apostle Thomas, one of the twelve. So let us turn attention to him. There is in the south of India a widely held tradition that this Thomas reached that country in the year 52 A.D., and established a Church, the descendant of which still exists (see essay *The rôle of Thomas*). It is very difficult to visualise that he might have initiated a tradition or text after leaving for such a remote place. It follows that the start of what we have may have been within less than one generation of the mission of Jesus.

The Church that Treasured the Gospel of Thomas

'A Christian gospel must have three essential constituents: Jesus, the Christ; the author of the gospel; and a church in which the gospel was nurtured, used, found useful, treasured and passed down to later generations.' ★ In this essay the rôle of that Church is looked at.

Recent research has established that at the time of Jesus there were a number of different ways in which the Hebrew religion was manifested, giving rise to various religious communities or almost different sects. This variableness has been especially brought to notice by the discovery of the Dead Sea Scrolls, the scriptures and rules of living of a monastic community at Qumran. Another aspect of this was that there was a distinction between those people who worshipped at the Temple in Jerusalem, and those out in the country who worshipped in synagogues. The former had a priesthood, the Holy of Holies containing the most sacred relics was within the Temple and no-one but the High Priest could enter it and then on only one day of the year, and animal sacrifices were performed at the altar. This was considered by all Jews to be at the centre of their religion, every Jew anywhere in the world had the obligation to pay to the Temple authorities two denarii each year—equivalent to two days' work—and it was important to make a pilgrimage there at least once in one's lifetime and for those living nearby to attend at the great celebrations. Such was its importance that Jesus regarded it as

★ The *Presentation*, page 3.

necessary to bring his mission to a conclusion there; and James and Peter considered that the first missionary activity had to start from Jerusalem itself.

The form of worship in the synagogues out in the country was different, apparently much more like that in synagogues all over the world nowadays. Instead of a priesthood, the lead was taken by a rabbi, serving more as a teacher and one who expounded the Law and the ways in which it was to be applied to daily life. Probably lay people assisted in the services. A symbolic ark contained the scroll of the Torah, which could be taken out and read from by others than the rabbi (Jesus read from it, *Luke 4:16–20*). Outward sacrifices had no place.

The real strength of the Hebrew religion lay in these synagogues and their worshipping communities. There were then about half a million Jews in Palestine, and twenty times that number in the Diaspora, spread about in many countries not only in the 'fertile crescent' of the eastern Mediterranean and Egypt, but extending into Asia, the Indus valley and southern India (the oldest synagogue still in use stands today near Cochin, its people maintaining the tradition that it was founded in the first century B.C.). This form of their religion remains of immense significance to the Jews of today, for it was in it that their religion was kept alive after the fall of Jerusalem in 72 A.D., with the total destruction of the Temple and the scattering of the priesthood.

However, Jews were only a minority, even in Palestine. The majority were otherwise. Very important amongst these were people of Hellenist background. These were the indigenous people, but their culture, their way of thought, and their religions were influenced by the great and ancient Greek civilization. They spoke a simplified form of the Greek language, which people in the City States regarded as barbaric—we call it the koine. They considered every natural event and every thing to be associated with some god or immaterial being, giving rise to the immense panoply of pantheism. While we would consider it to be cause and effect, they would, for example, think that it was in the nature of the spirit of a kettleful of water to make it boil when put over a fire.

Amongst these people, and it should hardly surprise us, were those who were not satisfied with that, and found a great attraction in the majesty of the Jewish concept of the one almighty God, who was just and fair, who had made a Covenant with his people, so these might find their right direction in life by living out their half of the contract. These people came into the synagogues. There they found a welcome, for those Jewish groups had a strong outgoing impulse to draw others into their communities. The Hellenists brought into these groups a practice that was normal to their communal lives—to permit the individuals to have a say in the running of affairs, something that is strange to many later Churches. Apparently, while the Hellenists could not hold the most solemn offices, they were otherwise fully accepted. It appears to have been a most extraordinary instance of toleration and acceptance of others.

As Jesus went about the country, giving total satisfaction at the deepest level to four or five thousand at a time 'besides women and children' (*Matthew* 15:38), speaking in Aramaic and no doubt Greek according to the needs of his hearers, some of those who had been worshipping in the synagogues wished to follow him. So a new Church came into existence.

This may be called a Hellenist synagogue Church. Its name does not really matter. What is relevant to this essay is that it took as its scriptures—upon which its doctrines and teachings were built—an early form of the Gospel of Matthew written in the Hebrew script, and an early form of the Gospel of Thomas. The former became known as the Gospel of the Hebrews. In due course the Church spread down to Alexandria, where a compatible gospel, referred to as the Gospel of the Egyptians, came into being. We now only know of the text of these gospels from the later quotations by the

Church Fathers, who regarded them as heretical in the sense of being condemned. It seems that Hebrews contained much that is in our Matthew's Gospel, while omitting a substantial amount (for it was about 90% the length), contained text that was removed from our Matthew, and had passages similar or identical to those in the Gospel of Thomas. Less is known about the Gospel of the Egyptians.

The people of Jewish race in this Church accepted Jesus as being the Messiah who had come upon the earth, they lived according to the Law, and they regarded the Holy Spirit as female (which relates to their referring to God as Mother). All its members saw Jesus as a teacher, as the embodiment of Wisdom, as a way, and not in a redemptive rôle. There was no call to emphasize the passion of Jesus and the resurrection of Christ.

There was perhaps a further factor. Certain of the great souls of the Greek civilization had recognized the concept of 'the human soul's entry into bodily incarnation and its eventual disengagement from the body', * to put it in a scholar's terminology. It has come down to us in the Prologue to John's Gospel, perhaps the most profound passage of text that has ever been written. Some of the more thoughtful or spiritually mature people in Palestine and surrounding lands might have been aware of this. They would have recognized this concept in the Gospel of Thomas, expressed as the Kingdom that is to be known within (*logion 3*), or the experience of reigning over the All (*logion 2*), where it is applied to each individual. It is easy to see that these people might have been drawn to join a Church based on such teachings, rather than any other of the new Churches.

In one respect the Hebrew religion of that time differed from its present attitude—it had a strong proselytizing element. As the Jews spread all over the lands of the middle

* Bentley Layton, *The Gnostic Scriptures*, page 366.

east and beyond they wished to draw others to join in their understanding of the great single God, who cared for, guided and judged them in their daily lives. They could assimilate into their worshipping communities those who were not of the House of Israel, of Jewish race. Furthermore, right from the very start, followers of Jesus wished to share what he had given them; they became and still are the most active of missionaries. Therefore there were in this early Church two motivations combining together to spread it out to others.

At a very early date, it seems, the apostle Thomas or his disciple Adonya—which may be abbreviated to Addai—had left Palestine and travelling north east on the trade routes reached Edessa on a tributary of the Euphrates, now called Urfa; it was then an important city, the Athens of the Orient, and had links from Greece to India. The later Acts of Thomas even say specifically that Jesus instructed him to go. There he converted and baptised the King Abgai, and established a Church. In due course, according to recent scholarship, this Church drew for support on the Church in Palestine, and grew into the Syrian Church.

Here then is the early Church that nurtured and treasured the Gospel of Thomas.

This Church which was founded by Thomas and his disciple Addai, with an admixture from an encratitic movement (see essay *Coloration*), existed from Syria through Palestine to Egypt. It continued for several centuries but was ultimately extinguished, its scriptures being destroyed as heretical and only few of its documents remain. However some have been discovered, usually in the form of copies from many centuries later. These will have been subjected to changes by successive redactors, but it is nevertheless possible to discern a coherent and consistent teaching of this Church such that it has been called the School of St Thomas.

The documents we now have from the later periods of this Church are known as The Acts of Thomas, the Hymn of the

Pearl, and the Book of Thomas. It is considered that these were written during the period 150 to 350 A.D., and almost certainly in Syriac, although Greek versions may have been produced simultaneously. The first two are now known in Syriac and Greek forms; the Book of Thomas was discovered in a Coptic version in the Nag Hammâdi Library.

The Acts of Thomas, like many other Acts of apostles or early saints, tell of the events and teachings of Thomas after he had begun his missionary activity. They tell of many episodes in the life of Thomas, incorporate concepts and even quotations from his Gospel, and give valuable insights into the rites of this early Church. Thus, adult baptism, preceded by an anointing (literally a 'Christing'), was the chief rite, and the eucharist took more the form of a love feast after an occasion of worship, apparently similar to that of the Sikh Church today. A significant element is that Jesus, as a living person, appears quite often in these episodes; at other times Thomas is likened to his twin, so they become also one. Most of the action take place to the east of Palestine, extending to north and south India, it being possible still to identify some of the other persons or places.

These Acts incorporate the Hymn of the Pearl, which appears at a stage in Thomas' mission when he was established in north India, at the court of King Gundaphoros. However, it is apparent from the nature of the writing that the Hymn is by a different author from the rest of the Acts; it can be only surmised whether it was incorporated by that first author or by a subsequent redactor.

The Hymn tells, in a form that could be chanted or even sung to music, the story of a prince living where the fertile valleys of the Euphrates and Tigris lead toward the Persian Gulf. A wonderful garment had been taken away from him, and to recover it he had to make the long journey by sea to Egypt, to search there for a pearl hidden in the Labyrinth near the pyramids, a place which mythically represented confusion and loss.   Stupefied by the strange food and rigours of the search, he nearly gave up and lay down to sleep.   His parents, discerning this from afar, sent to him an ambassador with a message that galvanized him to action.   He found the pearl and aided by a 'female being' returned to his home –

> 'But I could not recall my splendour;
> For, it was while I was still a boy and quite young
> that I had left it behind in my father's palace.
> But suddenly when I saw my garment
> reflected as in a mirror,
> I perceived it was my whole self as well,
> and through it I recognized and saw myself.
> For, though we derived from one and the same
> we were partially divided;
> and then again we were one, with a single form.' ⋆

So here is a particularly vivid and beautiful presentation of the key proclamation, given in many great spiritual teachings of the world, that a person, filled with the urge to find Truth, may start by searching outside, turning this way and that, but in the end recognizes that it not only lies within but has always lain within, previously unseen.

The Book of Thomas purports to be 'The hidden sayings that the saviour uttered to Judas Thomas, and which I, Mattaias, also wrote down.   I used to travel and listen to them as they were talking to one another.'   This at least gives the justification for the form of the writing, and illustrates the high regard paid to Thomas in that Church.   Thomas is presented as asking rather simple questions, which give rise to rather voluminous responses.   These do convey, or at least incorporate, a teaching, which has a mystical element combined with an ascetic approach.   There is a change of style mid-way, becoming more like a straight series of sayings each with an outer form and an inner meaning.

⋆ M R James, *The Apocryphal New Testament*, 1953, Oxford.

Certain features are common to these three works: they are presented in the style of an oriental story teller; there is much decoration and incidental description, as though pictures in words were being revealed; their expansiveness shows they are not direct words of a Master. The outward form is much emphasized, and the inner meanings could go unnoticed or be interpreted in significantly different ways. However, there is within each one a definite clue pointing towards the teachings as we have them in the Gospel of Thomas, sometimes there are direct quotations of, or at least close allusions to, its logia. For anyone interested, by taking up this clue a consistent series of inner meanings throughout each work can be discovered. It is a clear indication of how the aspirants for spiritual Truth were to find their reward in this Church.

Taking these three works (and there may have been others) it is possible to surmise how they, and the Gospel of Thomas, may have been used in the liturgy of that Church. In the first place, a single logion or a group of them with a common theme (as given in some of these essays) may have been taken as what are now called 'texts' upon which something like a sermon might have been based. More often, probably, they were used as a focus for contemplation by an individual. In both cases these would probably have led to sessions in which aspirants for spiritual Truth sat before one who has already made more progress, questioning and assimilating the answers. This is the way, sometimes the main way, in which spiritual Truth is communicated in almost all the major religions except Christianity. This difference between the small group of seekers sitting before one who has found, and the use of sermons within the liturgy, has been compared to tutorials and lectures in the academic environment.

Another document we have attributed to Thomas is the Gospel of Thomas such as may be found in books of the Apocryphal New Testament published up to the middle of this century. This is not unique in offering a series of incidents of the childhood of Jesus. He is shown doing miraculous deeds such as might befit a wonder child, or bringing blessings to people, or confounding his teachers. This short book has a rather sentimental nature, but a certain naïvity and charm. It must have attracted many of its hearers. It is difficult to think of it as being other than fictional, and it is not easy to discern significant spiritual overtones or qualities.

In considering this early Church, especially in Syria, it is also necessary to take into account the Diatessaron of Tatian. It is considered that this was written in about 170 A.D. and gives the appearance of being an amalgam or composite of the four Gospels of the Bible. However it has been subject to frequent amendment by redactors, a particular effect being to bring it more into harmony with the canonical Gospels when these had been translated into Latin probably by 384 A.D., the Vulgate. Professor Quispel refers to these versions as having been 'vulgatized'. It is in this connection that the authority on biblical writings, J Rendel Harris could write with the exuberance of a young man: 'since the Harmony is substantially a New Testament MS., it is impossible it could have remained in circulation without being affected by the same causes which were in operation to change the form of every successive recension of the New Testament into agreement with the latest recension of all.' However, by diligent comparisons, scholars can work out what certain key phrases or words might have been in the original versions. An important aspect of this is that Titian, in making his text, is now known to have had also a fifth source available to him, either the Gospel of Thomas or its precursor.

Titian's Diatessaron became the primary gospel used in the Syrian Church, and a major basis of the doctrines and teaching of that Church. Especially in the earlier versions of this that we have, a special use of the Biblical Greek word ΣῳΖῳ and its derivatives has been noted. Instead of this being 'to save', 'salvation' and 'the saviour', Syrian words meaning 'to live', 'life' and 'the life giver' are used; so Christ is spoken of as the Life Giver, meaning in the here and now. This may well have been of more significance than the single word we can note today. Consider that the World Council of Churches takes as its basis the acknowledgement of 'Our Lord Jesus Christ as God and Saviour', so that saviour-hood—with its concomitants 'saved from what?', 'by whom?' and 'in what way?'—goes along with the Creed; might that early Christian Church have had a teaching that would make that formula inappropriate?

As we become familiar with the Gospel of Thomas, with its primary emphasis on the indwelling Kingdom that may be known (*logion 3*) which leads to a sense of Oneness (*logion 22*), it is easy to visualize that it would encourage a mystical form of spiritual experience. By the fourth century the writings of Makarios displayed the flowering of the mystical Church of Edessa.

The indigenous Christians of India, that is to say not those following the Church of Rome brought there by the Jesuits in the sixteenth century nor the various Protestant Churches brought there since the time of the British Raj, include several derivatives of the Syrian Church, still owing their allegiance to the Eastern Patriarch. Amongst these there is the tradition that the Apostle Thomas came to the Indus valley, serving and converting King Gundaphoros. Much more emphatic is the living tradition of the Orthodox Church of Thomas in Kerala, in the extreme south west of that sub-continent. They assert he came there between 50 and 60 A.D.

During the great struggles between the early Christian Churches, which came to a climax during the fourth and fifth centuries, the Syrian Church and its derivatives passed into the background as far as the Churches of the west and the Russias were concerned. And the primitive Church that was the bearer of an independent tradition to that Syrian Church (however much it may have been modified subsequently) was extinguished. That extinction was so ruthless, so thorough, that only faint traces of it remain, needing all the resources of the latest scholarship to reveal. But the Gospel of Thomas, dug up from the sand, shines like a beacon to confirm the basic teachings on which it was built.

This essay has used conversations with Professor Gilles Quispel of Utrecht and Professor Joseph B Skemp of Durham and Bristol. Also the following sources –

G Quispel, *Gnostic Studies*, especially vol. II, 1975, Istanbul.

W H C Frend, *The Rise of Christianity*, 1975, London.

M R James, *The Apocryphal New Testament*, 1953, Oxford.

E Hennecke, *New Testament Apocrypha*, tr. R McL Wilson, 1963, London.

Bentley Layton, *The Gnostic Scriptures*, 1987, London.

A F J Klijn, *The Acts of Thomas*, 1962, Leiden.

J Rendel Harris, *The Diatessaron of Titian*, 1890, London.

A Vööbus, *Early Versions of the New Testament*, 1954, Stockholm.

C V Cheriyan, *A History of Christianity in Kerala*, 1973, Kottayam, India.

A S Atiya, *A History of Eastern Christianity*, 1968, London.

A special for Quakers

This essay is a special one for Quakers. It refers to concepts, and uses words, that are familiar to Quakers and touches on some themes that are of present-day relevance to them. These may not be clear to others—please may that be excused; just look on this with amusement, or perhaps amazement, or even with a certain marvelling *(logion 2)*. Because of the diversity of views held by Quakers, an attribute we value, anything written of them cannot be other than a personal contribution.

The justification for the essay is that the Gospel of Thomas and its background are particularly relevant to Quakers' approach to spiritual Truth and to their way of worship. Most Quakers in Britain have heard about the Gospel of Thomas; perhaps one third of them have read or heard quotations from it; it is thought that there is a copy of it in about one in ten of their homes. Of course, since there are now only 20,000 Quakers in Britain, the actual figures represented by those proportions are only very tiny.

The primary reason for this degree of familiarity with this Gospel is the emphasis given by every Quaker to be willing to consider any new insight into spiritual Truth. This is embodied in some of the Advices and Queries, * read in meeting for worship frequently enough for all to be familiar with them: ". . . Be ready at all times to receive fresh light from whatever quarter it may come; . . . Are you loyal to the

* Published 1964 by London Yearly Meeting of the Religious Society of Friends.

truth; and do you keep your mind open to new light, from whatever quarter it may arise? Are you giving time and thought to the study of the Bible, and other writings which reveal the ways of God? Do you recognize the spiritual contribution made by other faiths?"

Every Quaker owns that her or his Religious Society was founded by George Fox, even if this is to be quickly followed by the idea that things are different today and it is important not to be tied to the past. Very rarely is consideration given to his place amongst the great ones of humanity. We can accept that spirituality is the highest of human attainments, or a direct manifestation of the divine, and that the creation of a religious movement or Church is a particularly great form of this quality. Let us look at those who have served humanity in that way. We can easily start with Jesus, Moses, Krishna, Buddha, Mahomet, Guru Nanak (founder of Sikhism); go on to Socrates, Plato, Confucius, Plotinus; we would leave out Constantine, Alexandra the Great, Napoleon, Churchill as contributing at another level; we could add in St Francis, Luther, Joan of Arc, Wesley; some would count in Jung and Mother Teresa in this century. Whatever one does in this little ploy, it becomes necessary to include George Fox amongst perhaps the top twenty of mankind.

Here then is a spiritual giant. Only when he is seen in his stature, and we acknowledge our miniscule capability, can our debt to him be owned, and our responsibility as his heirs, after three and a half centuries, be properly carried forward in maintaining our Religious Society. Its early larger popular following was reduced by attitudes of exclusiveness and rigidity we now recognize as mistaken. But as the ecumenical process continues it may well have a distinctive contribution to give within the wider context of Christian Churches.

George Fox tells us that his mission was preceded by a series of great mystical experiences, his 'openings'. At their centre lay the experience of the indwelling Christ. For Fox, and for his followers who received enlightenment from him, this indwelling Christ had a power, a certainty, an assurance that contrasts strangely with the still small voice of God in our consciences that we now own to. Fox gave all his teaching in the language of the Bible, for it was the most important document of his day and invested with a real authority. Nevertheless, he was extremely selective in its use. Some passages he placed great weight upon; some he illumined so brilliantly that he is for us one of its finest exponents; some he explained away or transformed into something other; many he just ignored. Although he said that after his great openings he found many of them confirmed in the Bible—which we can see as rather charmingly naïve—he did not base his teachings on the Bible, he used the Bible to express his insights.

Great amongst these insights was his assertion that the truth being proclaimed was primitive Christianity regained, the teachings of the Apostles once again made known after a long night of apostasy. Here is the source of the Religious Society of Friends being termed Christian. It is a claim that is relevant today in the sense of a worshipping community established within a Christian ethos; there could be no confusion with Hindu, Moslem or Shinto. Yet emphatically it does not carry any sense of this being the only way. Certainly a person who has found satisfaction in any of the great religions or spiritual teachings may belong fully here, finding a community of good, sincere and kindly people, who know by experience that these different approaches are an important and valuable part of man's religious quest. Thus he or she may share in the worship with less need to turn a deaf ear or a blind eye to anything said or seen than in probably any other Church.

Within this context some present day Quakers, whose ideas come in all sorts of shapes and sizes, do not find it proper to call themselves Christians or consider they belong to a Christian Church. If they are more direct, they admit 'It depends what is meant by Christian'—and that is exactly the

point. Quakers may from time to time attend services in other
Christian Churches that acknowledge the Creed. Of one thing
we can then be sure: when it is said, most may stumble over
one or more of the phrases. We may explain this away by
asserting the unhelpfulness of trying to define such concepts
in words. But if we are honest, and take these phrases with
the meanings that other Christians use, we have to admit that
we cannot own to all of them.

From this quandary many Quakers turn to the idea of Jesus
being the one to follow. Without getting involved in any of
the Christology that sets theologians writing hundreds of
books, they seek out a vision, an awareness of the Perfect Man,
who in his dealings with people and situations reveals the
archetype of a man or woman rightly working through life.
He is a pattern, of whom they seek to become an image,
however imperfectly. In the quiet of a Quaker meeting for
worship, and within their own homes, they seek to discern just
what this might truly be, and how it affects their immediate
daily lives.

This awareness, this inner vision, may come through
worship. For confirmation, there can be no better touchstone
than the Gospels. Alas! there are many Quaker meetings for
worship that can go for weeks on end with no mention of Jesus,
no reference to the Bible. That cannot be in right ordering.
The fact is, within the Christian ethos, there can be no other
base.

George Fox had the Bible as his touchstone, even though
his spiritual insights often went beyond its words. He founded
a community seeking to emulate that of the Apostles. We
have also the Gospel of Thomas, which he did not have. We
know also of the primitive Church based on its teachings,
related texts and living traditions, which he could not turn to
as an example to emulate. Here surely is an opportunity to
be ready to receive fresh light, to be loyal to a truth revealed,
to open our minds, to give time and thought for study, and

to recognize a spiritual contribution coming from another direction.

Fox had 'Behold, the kingdom of God is within you' *(Luke 17:21)* to support his most basic experience; we now have 'The Kingdom is at your centre and is about you' *(logion 3)*. He had 'Abide in me, and I in you' *(John 15:4)*; we now have 'He who drinks from my mouth shall become like me; and I myself will become him' *(logion 108)*. The experiences that came to Fox, his proclamations to his people, his personality, his impact on those who saw and heard him, his example that released and inspired others, are all signs of his near complete absence of ego; we now have 'Become your true selves, as your ego passes away' *(logion 42)*.

Fox placed prime reliance on what was experienced within. We know the certainty that this, and this alone, can give—no matter how baffling it may appear to others. It cannot be different from–

> When you know yourselves
> then you will be known,
> and you will be aware that you are
> the sons of the Living Father. . . . *(Logion 3)*

Fox made much use of Paul's teachings such as the place of the cross, the sacrifice of Jesus, the cleansing rôle of his spilled blood, his atonement for our sins, even though he invested them with meanings and significance of his own. In their more accepted usages they are not easy for Quakers today so when they are associated with Fox, as now quite often happens, he is rejected also. As a way out of this confusion we can now see that they were not an integral part of that primitive Church.

On the other hand Fox, perhaps inspired by Margaret Fell, denied Paul's statement on the limited place of women in the Church, so we are freed from the predicaments the other Churches have got themselves into; we know week by week of their special spiritual sensitivity, and can now find the significance of the word 'mankind' encompassing both the male and the female, the underlying Oneness *(logion 114)*, to make sense of it all and avoid some modern extremes.

In that early Church the pattern of the Jews and those of Greek background, as members of the worshipping community, was remarkably similar to what Quakers mean when referring to members and attenders in our meetings. The absence of any priesthood, the rôles of lay people look little different from our elders and overseers. The welcome and tolerance then must have been just what we aspire to today. The approach where less reliance was placed on a proclaimed teaching and more on a contemplative seeking out of deeper meanings, is entirely familiar to us. The completion of a time of worship by the sharing of a meal, each bringing however little or much to be shared, reminds us of any Monthly Meeting tea; some of our worshipping groups even have an occasional 'eating-meeting'.

We can easily share the awareness of the wonder of a new life *(logia 4 and 50)*, or the 'Place where the beginning is, there will be the end' *(logion 18)* at our passing. We know that 'There is light at the centre of a man of light, and he illumines the whole world. If he does not shine, there is darkness' *(logion 24)*.

In the middle of this century Quakers led amongst all other Churches in coming to terms with sexuality within the context of modern medical science. This great instinct can take its proper place, and not release its power in the excesses either of licentiousness or of the encratitic element in that primitive Church. The rightful component of that movement, to recognize simplicity and to avoid a lust for material things with its exploitation of the natural world, has been demonstrated by Quakers over three and a half centuries.

Most Quakers are very literate, both as writers and more especially as readers. Nevertheless we know that importance lies not so much in the words and phrases themselves as in the awareness that comes through them and exists beyond. Thus it has been said that one of the special, even unique, qualities of the Gospels of the Bible is that they permit Jesus to become known as a friend. Now we have the Gospel of Thomas, recording additional and significantly different sayings from him, adding almost an extra dimension.

Certainly the spiritual import of these sayings does not jump out easily from the pages. Many of them are difficult in themselves, and others lead us on a journey during which much of our accumulated luggage must be discarded. Added to this, the experience of some who have used the Gospel of Thomas shows that too intense attention on the actual words may produce a block. It is necessary to try to rise above that, to soar a little beyond; and in making that jump we can have the beckoning and support of one we know as a friend. It is in our times of worship, in our practised silent contemplation amidst a group whom we trust and know will always support us, that this may most easily happen. 'It is only in the act of contemplation, when words and even personality are transcended, that the pure state of the Perennial Philosophy can actually be known.' *

Thus every Quaker places foremost in her or his evaluation the experience of the meeting for worship. But many feel a questioning, even an anxiety, about the lack of substance being expressed today. Let us work to be true heirs to the insights of that spiritual giant and founder of a worshipping community, without cutting adrift from our foundations. And add to that a greater awareness of the teachings of Jesus brought into the open by a chance discovery, and the recognition of a whole Church brought into the open by modern scholarship.

* Introduction by Aldous Huxley to *Bhagavad-Gita*, trans. Swami Prabhavananda and Christopher Isherwood, 1947, page 6, Phoenix House, London.

The rôle of Thomas

'A Christian gospel must have three essential constituents: Jesus, the Christ; the author of the gospel; and a church in which the gospel was nurtured, used, found useful, treasured and passed down to later generations.' In this essay the rôle of Thomas is looked at.

The person we first have to consider is the apostle Thomas, we will see how far that takes us. John's Gospel names him 'Thomas called the twin' (20:24). This twin-ship is emphasised in the introductory logion of the Gospel of Thomas, where its writer is said to be Didymos Judas Thomas, because both 'Didymos' and 'Thomas' in Greek mean 'twin'. It is obvious that this person was not born as the twin of Jesus, nor was he Judas (or Jude, the same Greek word) the blood brother of Jesus told of by Mark (6:3). It almost certainly means a form of spiritual twin. For many centuries there was a tradition in the Russian Orthodox Church that the apostle Thomas had a special affinity with Jesus, and in their ikons he is portrayed with a particularly sensitive expression. A similar tradition must have reached Leonardo da Vinci, who places him beside Jesus in his great fresco of the Last Supper. In the Gospel, logion 13 reveals him in a distinctive relationship in this regard. Having shown that he was aware of being before one whose resemblance it was impossible for him to express, it was he who was taken on one side in order to be given three logia, expressing a most high level of spiritual Truth.

Jesus said to his disciples:

Make a comparison to me and tell me whom I resemble.

Simon Peter said to him:
You resemble a righteous angel.
Matthew said to him:
You resemble a wise man, a philosopher.
Thomas said to him:
Master, my mouth will actually not accept
saying who you resemble.
Jesus said: I am not your master;
because you have drunk,
you have become drunk from the bubbling spring
which I have made to gush out.
And he took him,
he withdrew, he spoke three logia to him.
Now, when Thomas had returned to his companions,
they questioned him: What did Jesus say to you?
Thomas said to them:
If I tell you one of the logia that he said to me,
you will take up stones and throw them against me;
and fire will come forth from the stones and burn you up.

We know from the other Gospels that this incident must
have taken place when Jesus was travelling about with his
immediate disciples, rather than with great crowds. There
have been many instances, well authenticated, where a Teacher
with much spiritual discernment can recognise that a particular
follower is ready to receive more, even though others are not
ready. So the two go off to a private place, where the
additional Truth can be conveyed, and enlightenment given.
It is clear enough that this is what happened here.

Thomas is referred to particularly in John's Gospel, but
suggestions have been made that two separate mis-translations
have occurred which affect the attitude we may have towards
him. With respect to the first, M Phillipe de Suarez [1] suggests

that John's Gospel refers five times to Thomas as 'the disciple
who Jesus loved'.   In 13:23 at the Last Supper he was close to
Jesus—as portrayed by Leonardo—and able to hear, so Peter
asked him who it was that Jesus meant would be the betrayer,
before the morsel of bread was dipped and given to Judas
Iscariot.   In 19:26–27 Jesus on the cross commended this
disciple to his mother as her son, and he took her home with
him.   In 20:2 Mary Magdalene, finding the tomb empty, ran to
where Peter and this disciple were.   And in 21:7 it was this
disciple who identified Jesus when he appeared to seven of them
while fishing, and told them where to cast their net to fill it.

Suarez goes on to suggest that the fifth reference to this loved
disciple, which is so puzzling in our Bible, is due to a mis-
translation.   In the 21st chapter of John, Peter has been
questioned whether he loves Jesus deeply enough, and is urged
by Jesus to "tend my sheep".   Then Suarez would make John
21:20–22 read thus:

> Peter turned and saw following them the disciple whom
> Jesus loved, who had reclined close to him at the supper
> and said, "Lord, who is it that is going to transmit your
> [teaching] to posterity?"   When Peter saw him, he said
> to Jesus,"Lord, what about this man?"   Jesus said to
> him, "If it is my will that he remain until I come, what is
> that to you?   Follow me!"

The difference lies in the verb at the end of verse 21.   The
Greek ΠΡΟΔΙΔΩΜΙ gives the usual rendering 'to betray'.   But
ΠΑΡΑΔΙΔΩΜΙ means 'to transmit, to deliver to posterity', a
simple enough change to have been made during the redactions,
accidentally or on purpose.   And he gives the literal translation
of the clause as 'who is it that will transmit you to posterity?'
He adds that the parallels in Mark 14:19 and Matthew 26:22
support this version.

To set against this, there is the idea—so deep seated that it
comes out automatically—that this apostle is the Doubting

Thomas. Without a moment's thought, it causes ever so many people to doubt the Gospel of Thomas. It comes from John's Gospel 22:19–29, which most expert commentaries maintain to be an addition to the original text. After his crucifixion, Jesus had appeared to some of the disciples, but Thomas was not with them. On being told, he would not accept their word. Eight days later Jesus came again and then urged Thomas to feel his hands and side. The response of Thomas we are usually given is to exclaim "My Lord and my God!" However, this is where the second mis-translation may have occurred, for F C Burkett [2] has suggested the meaning of Thomas' words may be "It is Jesus himself, and now I recognise him as Divine." The following text referring to belief does not relate well with such a recognition, nor can we feel certain, after reading the Gospel of Thomas with its emphasis on knowing and absence of mention of belief, that Jesus would have asked Thomas to believe.

So far we have been using comparisons between the various Gospels, a technique so diligently used by many writers. Let us try another approach. It is well known by any teacher or lecturer that if a number of hearers are asked what was said, many different replies will be given. It is not just a matter of lack of concentration or forgetfulness. Much more significant is the capability of each hearer to understand what was spoken. One who is in a good position to understand will be the more likely to have grasped the exact meaning, the nuances of the wording, of what was being presented. We have already seen that the Gospel of Thomas has very precise wording, words cannot be altered, added or taken away without impairing the significance of what is there. It follows that the first hearer of the words from Jesus must have been well attuned to him. However, if we read this Gospel or the others in the Bible with open eyes, we will find that one of the recurring themes is that so many of his hearers did not understand Jesus. So there must have been something special about whoever it was that heard these words, the initial and prime messenger to us—the first one to transmit this teaching to posterity. We do not know of anyone better qualified than the apostle Thomas to have done this.

There is another clue, a subtle one. The only direct reference to Thomas as the first messenger of these words is in the Introduction to this Gospel, a straight-forward statement that may well have been added by the final redactor. There is no overt claim of being in any special position to understand what was being said, of being in any privileged condition. The only thing like this is logion 13, where the consequence of having been told something of Truth was to qualify the hearer for ritual execution by stoning. These all point to that first person being devoid of ego; that is to say, at an advanced stage on the way towards awareness of spiritual Truth. That awareness, combined with absence of ego, is not much evident amongst the other men disciples as recorded in the Gospels, even though they got to it later. (Did you notice the qualifier 'men'? Mary sister of Martha, Mary Magdalene pouring her ointment, Mary the mother of Jesus, Salome, the Samaritan woman at Jacob's well, are all shown to be thus favoured.)

And no-one with absence of ego would have fabricated or falsified the words of his Master who released him from darkness into light.

We cannot tell what rôle the apostle Thomas might next have played. In those days people had much better memories than we have with our reliance on documents. The Jews had, and still have, an intense tradition that no word, not even a jot or tittle, of holy writ may be changed. That carried over into respect for the remembered and spoken words of Truth. So Thomas might have remembered what he had heard, carrying it in memory for several years. It may have been passed on to others in this oral form; it may even have been carried thus to Edessa to be finally written down perhaps a century later. But it is just as likely that it may have been committed to writing quite soon. In every sizeable market place there were scribes, to whom the sayings could have been dictated. Here, again we have to take into account the precision of the wording as we have it. One of the things that happens in oral transmission is that, although the significant or important phrases and words remain intact, additions or glosses are made. In particular, these are to help in understanding meaning, or to create an atmosphere for what is to be said. It is noticeable how free the Gospel of Thomas is of these.

It is also proper to consider what Thomas might have done with respect to the language used. There is no question that the idiom of very many of the sayings is Semitic—short phrases, often repeating an idea with variations or contrasts, very closely related to the human and country scene observed by a keen eye. They are very distant from Greek speech, with its constructed sentences. So some scholars say the tradition for the Gospel was transmitted to Edessa in either the western Aramaic that Jesus spoke as his mother tongue, or as the closely related eastern Aramaic spoken in Edessa. However, scholars are clear that the Gospel of Thomas as we have it started as a complete text in Greek. Most certainly it was a Greek version that was translated into Coptic, because so many of the words—important ones— are left in Greek. But that is not to say that Thomas, or anyone else, translated the words of Jesus from Aramaic into Greek. Jesus himself might have spoken all these sayings in Greek, and Thomas might just as certainly have understood, remembered and either passed on or dictated them in Greek.

Now we need to take into account other events that might have happened to Thomas. First, in the Doctrines of Addai [3] we have a record, supported by other traditions or references, that Addai a disciple of Thomas took his teachings to Edessa (now Urfu) in Mesopotamia, and established the forerunner of the Syrian Church. Thomas may have travelled with him. At any rate, there is clear evidence that Thomas became greatly revered in that Church.

Second, in the Acts of Thomas [4] —a work written in the fourth century and worded rather much as a story-teller would do—one of the first episodes is that Jesus, it is implied having survived his crucifixion, wanted Thomas to take the Message to the East. Thomas protested, so Jesus sold him as a slave to a trader. In due course he reached the kingdom of Gundaphoros, which is thought to have been in the valley of the Indus. Here, because of having the skill of a carpenter and being able to construct the roofs of buildings with long spans of timber, he was engaged to build a palace for the king. This links up with an independent tradition, that by about the year 46 A.D. Thomas was serving king Gundaphoros.

There is also some evidence that the year 52 was also significant in two respects. One is that the apostles may have returned to Jerusalem then to honour the passing of Mary the mother of Jesus. The second that it may have been the date of the gathering of apostles to consider the rightness of Paul's teaching and doctrines (Acts ch. 15). Anyway, whether those were relevant, there is a very strong tradition [5] that by the year 52 Thomas reached Muziris (now Cranganore) on the Malabar Coast of south-west India and started to establish his apostolic Church. It is known Jews were then settled there, and the oldest synagogue, dating from that period, still stands in nearby Cochin and is in use. The traditions tell of Thomas having a difficult time to begin with, but slowly winning acceptance, including support of important people, until he had set up seven churches in places that can be identified. He then moved over the hills towards the east, going near to what is now Madras, setting up more churches until finally he was martyred in 72 A.D. His tomb is still venerated, with a big celebration each year. That whole Church, now called the Apostolic Church of Thomas, is linked to five other Eastern Orthodox Churches, and is very much alive although probably rather different in its doctrines and liturgy from its early days.

We have a witness to those early events from an ancient Syriac document which summarized the missionary activites of the original apostles and reads –

> 'India, and all the countries belonging to it and round it, even to the farthest sea, received the apostles' ordination to the priesthood from Judas Thomas, who was guide and ruler in the Church which he had built there, in which he also ministered.' [6]

Admittedly much of this is based more on traditions than what we usually regard as firm evidence—it has to be remembered that the Indian monsoon renders all documents useless within a very few years, and the lush tropical vegetation quickly engulfs unkempt buildings. On the other hand, generally in Indian culture reliance is placed more on living traditions than on written documents. Thus taken together it poses a very firm possibility that Thomas started off his Gospel, in either a clear oral form or, more likely, a written form, before he went out to India. That is to say within not more than 15 or 20 years of the ministry of Jesus. This makes it earlier than, by general consent, the dates of the other books of the New Testament.

[1] *L'Évangile Selon Thomas*, 1975 version, Éditions Métanoïa, page 260.

[2] *The Gospel History and its Transmission*, 3rd edition, 1911 (Quoted in Encl. Brit. 14th edition, vol. 13, page 25d, 1929).

[3] *Doctrina Addai*, ed. Philips, A.N.C.L., 1876.

[4] *The Acts of Thomas*, A F J Klijn, 1962, Brill.

[5] *Kerala, a portrait of the Malabar Coast*, G Woodcock, 1967, Faber and Faber.

[6] *The Ante-Nicene Fathers*, A Roberts and J Donaldson, vol. VIII, page 671, Edinburgh; and W B Eerdmans Publishing Co, Michigan, 1968.

48

The Words of a Master

Try an experiment. Choose a logion, or even part of one,
that appeals to you. Write it out in longhand on a card, taking
care to do it tidily and without mistakes (just in case these are
the words of Jesus). Put the card on your mantlepiece or stick
it on the reminder-board in your kitchen for a few days. Then
it will catch your eye, and the words will be recalled to mind.
See whether there is some strange growth in the significance
of the saying, as though something is maturing within you.

If this experiment works for you, you will have discovered
at first hand what distinguishes the words of a Master from
ordinary words; and you will have discerned something of
what it is that permits one of these very special people to be
regarded as a Master.

·   ·   ·   ·   ·   ·   ·

A Master does not need to be a spiritual Master. They can
be active in other fields. Winston Churchill was able to give
resolution to his people to withstand the prospect of invasion
by a nation ruled by a despot, when all alone at a crucial stage
of the second world war. Leonardo da Vinci and Raphaël
were masters in the field of art, Mozart of music. Shakespeare
saw to the depths of personality and expressed it in drama and
words. However, the spiritual being the highest manifestation
of the capacity of mankind, a spiritual Master must be
supreme. The words of such a one are what we have in the
Gospel of Thomas.

·   ·   ·   ·   ·   ·   ·

There are other criteria that distinguish the words of a Master from those of others. One is that they are extremely carefully chosen, they are very exact for the meaning they are intended to convey. Another way of looking at this is that if any of the words were to be changed, something would be lost, or even the meaning changed. This showed up during the translation of the Gospel of Thomas; even allowing for the fact that the work was done from an earlier translation into the Coptic language, which is itself a 'dead' language today, it was found that very great precision in the choice of the English words, each with its connotations, was needed.

Another consequence is that the words are very few—the maximum content is expressed in the minimum of words. If they are very carefully chosen to give the intended meaning, what would be the value of adding anything more? This is one of the guide-lines used by scholars in attempting to discern the authenticity of early writings, especially when making comparisons between the four Gospels of the Bible. Words or phrases that appear to have been added, become of suspect authenticity.

However, there is an even more important factor that must be taken into consideration. In the Gospel of Thomas we have over one hundred sayings, with the possibility that they come fairly directly from a Master. That being so, despite their variety, they come from one source. Therefore it follows that they must have a homogeneity; in particular, there can never be a clash between one and another. This has important consequences in connection with coming to an understanding of the meanings of the 'difficult' logia. If any one of these is taken alone, it will probably be found that several different meanings may come to mind. But that will not do if they are the words of a Master—then the meaning of each saying has to be compatible with the meanings of all the others. This has been important in coming to the meanings that are presented in the Paraphrases and the Notes of the *Presentation* of this Gospel.

Finally, we have the situation that there are, and throughout the ages have been, only very few Masters, and many of these have not committed their words to writing. So we have very little practise at reading them. Each of us is dealing with a new experience as we come before the words of a Master; it behoves us to regard them with an awe and reverence, and through that allow them to do their intended work of growing within us.

.   .   .   .

The words of a Master are pure, are distilled and concentrated—a quality that may be likened to a strong spirit or a heavenly scent. When this is discerned, it is a sign of authenticity.

It is well worth working to be able to recognize the words of a Master. There is the obvious reason; but, in addition, it gives a touchstone to separate the wheat from the chaff. All too often discussion of spiritual topics rests on some detailed analysis of texts, or on cleverly constructed arguments. It is a welcome change from these to come on the words of a Master, then all the cobwebs are blown away.

Authenticity of the Gospel of Thomas

What is the basis for the authenticity of a document from antiquity? By what means can it be determined how that which is written is authentic?

This is a topic that indeed exercises those who work on the books of the Bible. Most often the first line of approach is to compare the document with others. The comparison may cover passages or even single words. The assumption is made—and it can only be an assumption—that where there is agreement there is greater authenticity. In the Gospels of the Bible this has led to the whole 'synoptic' idea, whereby the first three are compared and seen to be related in certain respects. This has been developed over the last century or two, but it is not taking into account the tendency of eighteen previous centuries, especially the earlier ones, to align or harmonize those Gospels. In effect, all these diligent studies are largely going backwards over the work of the various redactors, identifying those elements they harmonized. To some extent at any rate, the agreements reflect the success of the earlier harmonization, which is something quite different from establishing authenticity.

For the Gospel of Thomas, many scholars have made these comparisons, and identified quotations or equivalents from other writers of antiquity, or of passages from the Gospels of the Bible. ★ Strangely, however, these do little to establish any criteria by which authenticity might be determined, there

---

★ A good summary is given in *Évangile Selon Thomas*, Gillabert, Bourgeois and Haas, 1979 version, Éditions Métanoïa.

are differences that undermine conviction. Furthermore, it is
necessary to take into account an entirely different factor. By
the third century this Gospel was being branded as heretical
by the Churches that were claiming orthodoxy. This attitude
hardened, until a few centuries later any references to it were
deemed to be sinful. It is only to be expected that the basic
data upon which such comparisons could be made were being
destroyed. So, despite this approach being the one most
commonly used in the literature on the Gospel of Thomas, it
cannot serve its primary purpose of establishing authenticity.
It is necessary to follow other approaches.

It is valid to consider what is in the Gospel itself. One
aspect of this relates to the form or nature of the sayings.
These are very precise and terse. Their brevity is apparent;
the precision showed up especially in the translation. Often,
where alternatives might have been used for a particular word,
it was found that only one choice gave the most significant
meaning. It is this sort of concentrated meaning and precision
that is to be expected of the words of a Master; and it is just
this kind of detail that is likely to be blurred and lost when
teachings are passed down for too many generations orally, or
if written texts have been worked over too many times.

Consideration may also be given to the form in which the
Gospel became available for its final written composition,
which may have been in about the year 140 or earlier. On the
one hand, peoples' memories then were more acute than ours,
because our availability of printed records makes it less
important to remember precisely. It is just possible that the
sayings, the phrases and even words had been passed down for
three generations, as oral traditions. However, in that process
it is very likely that, although the main point may be recalled,
either phrases would be embellished or words blurred. But
we have already seen that the wording in our Gospel is very
precise. Furthermore, all of the sayings are very direct and

many of them are difficult; therefore there would have been every excuse to add explanations, which in fact has not happened.

In exactly the same way, the person who first heard or wrote these sayings, whether he was Thomas or not, would have been very unlikely to devise such precise and difficult phrases. He would have taken a less arduous line; only a Master takes his followers to the steepest part of the path.

Ultimately, authenticity is a matter for the individual. Depending on his background, he may prefer to accept the view of someone else, in effect to delegate the decision to a scholar, an ecclesiastic or another writer from antiquity. Or he or she may wish to establish that authenticity directly within. There are people who, as they become more familiar with the Gospel of Thomas, find that it has a self-authenticating quality.

54

A Heretical Gospel

"This Gospel [of Thomas] was branded as heretical by
Hippolytus, bishop of Rome, in the early third century."
(The Introduction to the *Presentation*). What was the significance of a bishop of Rome, and of the third century? What
does heretical mean? What were, and are, the consequences
of that branding? Is the Gospel heretical? What does that
mean to us?

By the second century of our era, the movement to set up
groups following the teaching and example of Jesus had
developed into the formation of four great Churches, centred
on Alexandria, Antioch, Byzantium and Rome. Furthermore,
within each of these there had been established hierarchical
structures, one comprising the clergy and the lay people, and
second among the clergy themselves. Hippolytus, who died
in 236, was at that time the head of the Church of Rome.

It has been a characteristic of Christianity to attempt to
formulate in words the concepts that its members consider
important. While this has generally been the case, it has not
been so in every instance—for example the Roman Catholic
Church attaches importance to certain attributes that are
maintained and passed on in intangible ways, and the Quakers
set little store by putting their understandings into verbal
formulæ. Nor, to an even greater degree, is it general to all
religions, for in the Hindu religion the verbal formulations—
particularly in writing—are very secondary to its expression in
the lives of its great sages and teachers; and likewise for other
Eastern religions.

Within those four great Christian Churches the clergy and theologians entered enthusiastically into the formulation of their understandings of their religion. In part this was to make it possible to distinguish who was a follower—that is, a member of the Church—and who not; and it gave people a certainty when faced with opposition. In part it must also have been able to help to establish their own status, for it is the rôle of one in authority to declare a position and he needs some formulation of it in order to be able to do that. Perhaps also it was just an enthusiasm, related to the coming together of many men with high intellectual capability. It may also be noted that by the fourth century (rather later) the Church of Rome was less concerned with the development of doctrines than the Byzantine Church.

Inevitably, those formulations developed differently. Then a second characteristic of Christianity came into play—to consider one view correct or right, and a different view erroneous or wrong. Again, this is not general to all religions, for Hinduism in particular not only accepts differing interpretations but positively welcomes them as being necessary to understanding Truth and also to meet the needs and capabilities of different people. This view of what is right and what wrong is moreover coloured by the assumption that one's own view is the right.

All this was becoming quite firmly established by the third century.

"The original meaning of the word 'heresy' was neither abusive nor complimentary. It came from the Greek *haereus* meaning an 'act of choosing' and then 'the choice of philosophical principles' and 'those who professed them' i.e. as a 'school or sect'." * But Paul and then the first century Churchman Ignatius began to apply it to views that they

---

* Joan O'Grady, *Heresy*, 1985, Element Books, pages 4 and 5.

considered would be disruptive to their own understanding of what Christianity meant. Thus it came to carry the overtone that it generally has today, of something that is at least erroneous and perhaps to be condemned.

An important aspect of this use of the word is that in order for there to be a heresy there must be an orthodoxy. And we have seen that the two essential requirements—an established doctrine, and the view that 'my idea is the right one'—were existing by the time of Hippolytus.

A more open-minded consideration will show that this use of the term heresy is to a significant degree relative. At the time of any of those formative arguments, each side must have considered its own view the orthodox, and the other heresy. This could only be resolved when one of the views had become widely established as a common consensus. This certainly was not a proper position for the Church of Rome to adopt at that time, when it was a relatively junior member of the four.

Of course the significance of what is orthodox and what heretical is much influenced by who wins out in any struggle. It is the view of the winner that becomes the orthodox view; he writes the history books (and controls subsequent theological discourses), and establishes the general view held through the centuries.

A singularly unfortunate corollary of this attitude of mind, represented by the change in the meaning of the word heresy, was first the addition of intolerance and then of persecution. Thus, when a Church was deemed to be heretical, in due course—sometimes soon, sometimes later—the leaders were driven out, the churches and their sacred possessions destroyed, followers driven into the wilderness or killed, and their libraries destroyed. One instance of this was the Donatists around Carthage in north Africa in about 310 A.D. Their leader Donatus was charged with ecclesiastical offences at a trial of rival bishops, confirmed in his 'guilt', and the power of the Roman state directed against his movement and followers who were no longer considered merely heretics but also rebels.

This example is one of many. It is mentioned because it is easy enough to imagine that it may have provided the spur to the monks at the Nag Hammâdi monastery to have buried treasures from their library, including the Gospel of Thomas. Scholars consider this took place in the early fourth century— and there was a Roman garrison across the Nile from their monastery.

With respect to the Gospel of Thomas, it must have been regarded as heretical by other Churchmen than Hippolytus, and until a later date—for we find them referring to it, always in condemnatory terms, in the third and fourth centuries. The reaction must have led to effective searches for every copy of it, so they might all be destroyed—for the only manuscripts we have are the very mutilated Oxyrhyncus version and the complete Coptic version.

This branding as heretical has not entirely lost its power to this day, as may be shown by an experience of the present author. The Anglican vicar of his village was a model of everything one might hope for. An earlier rendering of the Gospel of Thomas was offered to him and received with great appreciation and interest. It does not happen to every vicar to have someone in his parish, though not of his flock (although we are very ecumenical), who is translating a Gospel from an ancient manuscript. A few days later he wrote that on consulting his textbooks he had found mention of a gospel of this name having been considered heretical by Hippolytus, and might it be the case that this was the same gospel? The answer was given that undoubtedly it was; whereupon all interest evaporated.

Now we should turn to consider at greater depth why this condemnatory attitude to heresy developed. We have seen that one element may have been related to power within authority, which modern psychology has shown to have great significance.   Especially when it works at the unconscious level, it can manifest in many ways, some heavily disguised.

However, there is probably a more substantial aspect. Among the early Christian Churches there were many variants. Some of these seem to have been somewhat eccentric, or following lines of thought without much promise.   But Joan O'Grady shows that there was a common thread or factor running through many of them which, particularly, is to be contrasted with what became the orthodox Church.   This latter was working towards a truly catholic Church, using that term to mean 'for everyone'.   To this end it formulated definite dogmas, which its followers could adhere to, could be used as a touchstone of adherence, and as doctrines could be readily taught.   We can see the start of this in the Epistles of Paul, in the records of the teaching of the earliest apostles collected in the New Testament, in the 'slants' of our Gospels of Mark and of Matthew in particular.   It went on through the early centuries, and became established in the great Creeds, still in use.   An important feature of these is the acceptance of a single body of belief and faith in it which, for all those going along with it, serves as the basis of their religion.

Many of the other Christian Churches, on the other hand, did not wish to confine themselves to an approach appropriate 'for everyone'.   They recognized that for certain persons an alternative approach might be of value.   This was considered to be at a higher level;   to attain it a period of preparation in life would be needed, guidance obtained from one already at that level, and substantial effort and dedication given.   By this approach a more satisfying awareness, at a deep personal level, to spiritual Truth might be found.   And, being thus found, it could be manifested in daily living.

This kind of approach was not unique to these Christian

Churches. In fact, rather the contrary, for it was analogous to the way of other religions such as those known as the mystery religions, which were widespread at that time. These, being non-Christian, gave opportunity for the catholic Churches to criticize this alternative approach.

Nor has this kind of alternative been limited to that period and those Christian Churches. Today those who are wishing to seek this higher or deeper personal spirituality may do so through the Hasidim of the Hebrew religion, the Muslim Sufis, within Buddhism and the Zen religions and, most particularly, in the Vedanta branch of the Hindu religion. In all these religions these alternative approaches are recognized and welcomed, as meeting most effectively the differing spiritual needs of people.

The sad thing is that in those early centuries the Christian Churches developed antagonisms towards the alternative approach. The Gospel of Thomas is perhaps the finest record we have of what lay at the heart of one of these 'alternative Christian' Churches. It was branded as heretical in the condemnatory sense. If we can recognize that the term 'heresy' can also mean an alternative, then this Gospel may rightfully be called heretical, but giving us the opportunity to discern a form of Christian spirituality that has been hidden from us through these intervening centuries, until it came forth from its hiding in the sand.

The Unacceptability of the Gospel of Thomas

It is inevitable that many of those persons who are committed to the established Churches, and likewise some scholars and theologians, will find the Gospel of Thomas unacceptable. The inevitability arises from interesting manifestations of depth psychology.

Scholars need to carry out their studies with the intellect, with proper attention to facts, and due application of established philosophical and intellectual criteria and traditions. Upon this much of our western civilization has been built.

Some of the passages in the Gospel of Thomas cannot be grasped with the ordinary mind. Their meanings seem incomprehensible. In colloquial language they are gobble-de-gook or just plain nonsense. No matter how much we puzzle over them they cannot be made to make sense. Thus in logion 4 –

A man old in days will not hesitate
to ask a little child of seven days
about the Place of life,
and he will live,
for many who are first shall become last
and they shall be a single One.

How could many a professor consider for an instant that a little child could instruct him on the fundamentals of living? But if he has the fortune of seeing, with his inner eye, Perfection in the new-born baby his wife has presented him with, perhaps he may overcome the hesitation to go beyond his mind and find a higher level of Oneness whereby he will truly live.

Logion 7 is a direct assault on the intellect –

Happy is the lion which the man will eat,

and the lion will become man;

and abominated is the man who the lion will eat,

and the lion will become man.

To begin with, the lion is something symbolic—it is the 'little self' which contains within it all the pride in achievement of the mind. But worse, the first and the third phrases are reversed, so logic requires that the second and fourth should be also. But they are not. So the intellect says it must be a false copying by the scribe, an error in translation, a slip by the printer. But it is not. It is a technique by an oriental Master to force the aspirant after spiritual Truth to go beyond his mind.

In part of logion 61 –

Salome said: I myself am your disciple.

Jesus said to her: Because of that I say this:

When he is emptied

he will be filled with light;

but when he is divided

he will be filled with darkness.

How can a disciple reach the wonder of being filled with light by emptying himself? It is by discarding that little self with all its mind-made theories. And what obscuration results from being divided? And divided into what? The division is for him to be split between his little self and his true Self, his Oneness or individuation not found.

Since Jesus lived on earth the theologians of the Christian Church have developed doctrines to clarify its understandings and to serve as the basis of its teaching. As the Church became established with authority the acceptance of these as dogmas gave the distinctive mark of membership. Further, a very crucial development was the establishment of the hierarchical priesthood to give a structure and order to the Church. Both of these great trends may perhaps have been vital to its survival during periods of persecution and social disintegration. However, they have within them the factor of authority, which inevitably contains an element of the exercise of power.

In the Gospel of Thomas the revelation of spiritual Truth comes about through an individual's seeking with the assurance of finding. Thus from logion 2 –

> Let him who seeks not cease from seeking
> until he finds . . . .

and logion 92 –

> Seek and you will find.

That seeking needs to take a particular form –

> Know Him who is before your face,
> and what is hidden from you shall be revealed to you:
> for there is nothing hidden that shall not be manifest.
>
> *(logion 5)*

from which there is the great assurance that by the acceptance of what is offered a mutual indwelling shall be found –

> Jesus said:
> He who drinks from my mouth shall become like me;
> and I myself will become him,
> and the hidden things shall manifest to him. *(logion 108)*

All this is independent of any external authority. That is to say it is dependent neither on the work of the theologian nor on the doctrine of mediation by any other person. Is it not inevitable that such an undermining of influence will make this Gospel psychologically unacceptable?

Any person who is committed to an established Christian Church has built up his or her position within a background of believing and being a believer, of faith and being one of the faithful. Deeply ingrained, through frequent repetition in many guises, are the concepts of some inherent sinfulness from which the person is to be saved by a redemptive saviour.

None of these concepts appear in the Gospel of Thomas. Instead, what is given is summarized in logion 3—right near the beginning –

> If those who guide your being say to you:
> "Behold the Kingdom is in the heaven",
> then the birds of the sky will precede you;
> if they say to you: "It is in the sea",
> then the fish will precede you.
> But the Kingdom is at your centre
> and is about you.
> When you know yourselves then you will be known,
> and you will be aware that you are
> the sons of the living Father.
> But if you do not know yourselves
> then you are in poverty, and you are the poverty.

These sayings are expanded upon later in the Gospel, so telling us that it is from spiritual impoverishment that we are to be released; that this release comes about by seeking and finding such that one comes to know one's true Self at one's centre, and that it is there that the Kingdom or spiritual Truth is experienced.

Such a reversal from much to which a deep commitment has been given to something utterly different will inevitably be unacceptable. The Gospel even addresses this directly (again from logion 2) –

> . . . and when he finds,
> he will be disturbed;
> and when he is disturbed,
> he will marvel . . .

So we can find strange ways of working round this clash within. One is when a scholar searches through his great collection of earlier writings, perhaps using a computer to help him, and finds a passage that corresponds to something in the Gospel of Thomas. This is interpreted as evidence that this Gospel was put together by an editor copying the earlier text. He does not stop to think whether Jesus might have spoken thus, since real truths arise spontaneously again and again.

Another appears in one of the most serious and fully worked-out criticisms of the Gospel of Thomas, which well illustrates all the foregoing elements. A professor at a leading theological university (it is kinder not to be too specific) has made a most thorough comparison of this Gospel with other Gnostic writings—a widespread alternative Church of the early centuries of our era—and with the Gospels of the Bible. Throughout, wherever the Gospel of Thomas is similar to the Gnostic writings it is assumed to be derived from them; and whenever it differs from the Biblical Gospels it is assumed to be a corruption. Whether those assumptions are true or not is immaterial to the present essay. What is significant is that they are assumptions. There is no discussion of those guiding themes or consideration whether possibly in each case the real position is the reverse. Furthermore, they are not even mentioned; instead it is left to the observant reader to discern them, and to see that they influence the choice of passages on which the comparisons are made.

In addition, there is use of phrases that carry a highly emotive value: "tendentious divergences", "tendentious reinterpretation", "the picture has been drastically altered", "saying torn out of its context", "construction has been shattered". Again, whether such strong words are justified for the points being made is irrelevant here. What is significant is that they are quite unnecessary and, further, they are alien to the scholarly and well-chosen tone of everything else in the book.

Surely it would have taken Carl Jung just a few minutes to recognize there here was an outward manifestation of a great struggle taking place in the unconscious.

It is only by becoming free from such psychological impediments, to be willing to discard old luggage collected on the journey, that one may expect to find what the Gospel of Thomas has to offer in one's search for spiritual Truth.

Is the Gospel of Thomas a Gnostic Text ?

It is often written that the Gospel of Thomas is a Gnostic Gospel. This is primarily because it was found amongst many other books that certainly are Gnostic, and it seems likely that the monastery at Nag Hammâdi was primarily following that tradition. The consequence among Church-people and theologians is that this Gospel is belittled or even dismissed.

The background to this derives from one of the great struggles that took place within the Christian Church during the early centuries. The Gnostic Church was to a certain extent a syncretic Church, that is to say it assimilated into itself some concepts and ideas that were current around it. These included some from the Greek mystery religions and much from the Hebrew religion. As the teachings of Jesus began to spread, especially towards Egypt, some of these could be assimilated too. On the other hand, it made significant contributions of its own.

In his remarkably valuable survey of eastern and western religions and spiritual movements, and their developments, Professor Trevor Ling ★ gives this summary of Gnosticism –

'At least since the time of the Persian Empire of Cyrus, C6th B.C., on through the time of the Greek empire of Alexander and his successors, C4th B.C., religious ideas and practices from India (mainly Hindu) and Persia (mainly Zoroastrian) had been spreading westwards to mingle with Greek and Minoan elements to form a new

★ *A History of Religion East and West*, T Ling, Macmillan, 1968, p. 169.

religious syncretism which was found throughout the Mediterranean world. One of the most outstanding products of this is the family of cults and doctrines known as Gnosticism. The basic theme of Gnosticism was that of escape from the present material world, which was regarded as basically evil, the creation of a demiurge or inferior god, into another sphere where it would be possible to enjoy the full life of the spirit, a sphere which was held to be the true home of the divine spark within man. How to attain this higher, spiritual realm was the concern of the various Gnostic cults; in general its attainment was believed to be by knowledge (gnosis) of a divine saviour who alone could affect the soul's release. Such salvation was for the 'spirit' of man; not for the flesh or the body. The flesh is evil, said the Gnostics, and only by breaking free from it can man find the life of the spirit, and return to his true home. He cannot break free himself; a divine saviour must come from above, from the realm of pure spirit down through the increasingly gross emanations which lie between the spiritual realm and the evil world, a savour who will rescue the soul of man and return it to its home. Knowledge of the saviour was the all-important requirement so far as men were concerned.'

Ling was writing before the texts found at Nag Hammâdi were fully assimilated, and it is possible that his words were influenced rather much by the writings of the early Christian adversaries of Gnosticism. It does not matter very much for our present purpose, but it might be well to add a passage that truly is Gnostic –

'For when they had seen him and heard him, he granted them to taste him and smell him and to touch the beloved Son. When he had appeared instructing them about the Father, the incomprehensible one, when he had breathed into them what is in the mind, doing his

will, when many had received the light, they turned to
him.   For the material ones were strangers, and did not
see his likeness and had not known him.   Again,
speaking new things, still speaking about what is in the
heart of the Father, he brought forward the flawless
world.' *

Perhaps the greatest positive quality of Gnosticism was its
emphasis on Gnosis.   Gnosis means the knowing, at the centre
of one's being and far beyond the level of the mind, of spiritual
Truth.   It is a conscious awareness of the ultimate spiritual
knowledge of which a man or woman is capable.   The
attainment of Gnosis gives an experience of there being no
need—or possibility—of seeking beyond it.   The word, Greek
of course, is allied to that profoundly significant word
METANOIA.   When Jesus began his ministry, Mark's
Gospel in the Greek tells how he walked beside the Lake of
Galilee and, seeing Peter and his brother in their boats, called
out 'Come, metanoia, and follow me'.   This word is often
mistranslated as 'repent' which is entirely misleading.   Jesus
called on these men to change their knowing at their centre;
they did, and their lives were transformed.   For a seeker after
spiritual Truth, with its transforming quality, there is great
value in the emphasis on Gnosis.

There was, and still is for those who might follow this path,
two aspects to the attainment of Gnosis.   The first is the
recognition that this attainment is a path which the seeker
follows.   He or she starts without that awareness, and comes
to the attainment.   This transition may not be sudden like a
'conversion', but gradual.   The entering into the attainment,
to a lesser or greater degree, is of immense significance to the
seeker, and something to be treasured and never treated
lightly.   Therefore it was associated with events which are

---

* From *The Gospel of Truth* quoted in *The Gnostics*, Tobias Churton,
  Weidenfeld and Nicolson, 1987, page 21, using the translation of *The Nag
  Hammadi Library in English* edited by J M Robinson, Brill, 1977.

mistakenly called 'initiations'. Other words mistakenly used in connection with Gnosticism are 'secret' or 'mystery'—for example, a secret knowledge or a mystery cult. The use of the term 'secret' is an error for 'hidden'. There was and is no secrecy about Gnosis; but it is a quality that is hidden within each one of us and is waiting to be awakened, to be brought into consciousness, or become revealed; it is latent. The use of 'mystery' as something mysterious is an error; rightly it refers to something that has an outward form and an inner meaning. Correctly, every parable of Jesus in the Gospels is a mystery. A Gnostic trod the path of spiritual attainment by one or more 'initiations', each leading to a greater awareness of something that did and does exist and is treasured inwardly, and which looks to an outsider as something 'secret' or a 'mystery'.

The second aspect relates to the transmission of Gnosis as a living experience from one person who has Gnosis (to whatever degree) to another seeking it. This transmission of spiritual Truth and the way in which is it done, was known equally to the Gnostic Church, and is in the present day to the Hebrew Hassidim, the Muslim Sufis, the Buddhists of Tibet and Hindu Vedantists. Strangely, it may not be much known in the Christian Churches.

The Gospel of Thomas is entirely attuned to all these positive features, and so it is very easy to see why it could have been in the library of a predominantly Gnostic monastery, and treasured to such a degree that it was included amongst the books that had to be hidden in the sand when persecution was pending.

However, there were other aspects of Gnosticism that were truly alien to the Gospel of Thomas. Perhaps foremost amongst these were its doctrines about the creation of the world and its nature, and about good and evil. In fact these were linked. The existence of a physical world in which there is so much suffering, and in which man can perpetrate so much

evil, could not be reconciled to its being the creation of one
good God.   So the concept, akin to one of the most
fundamental to Zoroastrianism, was followed that the spiritual
and the good was created by God and the material and evil by
another entity called the Demiurge.   The Demiurge was more
potent than the Devil of the Christian Churches, it was able to
create.   This led the Gnostics to forsake the material world.
It led to austerity and asceticism, to living the lives of hermits
or in communities shut off from the world, to celibacy and
foregoing family life.

Now, it is very easy to see that all these attributes of the
Gnostic Church ran directly counter to those being developed
in the early Christian Churches.   These wished all people to
be able to enter, on the basis of belief and faith—a truly
catholic Church, without any implication that there were
degrees of being a Christian.   They wished spiritual Truth to
be mediated by a priesthood.   They considered it important
to have an ecclesiastical structure that would provide direction
and strength against persecution.   Monotheism was vital, and
there could be only one Creator.   It was cardinal that the
goodness of the spiritual could live in the material world and,
however imperfect that was, could redeem it.   And the evil in
men's hearts was cleansed by the supreme sacrifice of Jesus.

The Gnostic Church in the early centuries had a wide and
numerous following.   It, and its teachings, became a serious
threat to the Christian Churches.   Thus they turned against it,
branded it as heretical, and persecuted it and its followers.   So
successful were they at this, that through the intervening
centuries almost everything known about the early Gnostic
Church has been from the writings of its adversaries.   It
is small wonder that there may have been misunderstandings.
In particular, at the present day, many who follow
orthodox doctrines automatically condemn anything to do with
Gnosticism.   One of the very special consequences of the find
of all those books of the Nag Hammâdi library is that only now

is a reappraisal of Gnosticism taking place, based on its own source documents.

Because Gnosticism, and its emphasis on Gnosis, contains important elements of spiritual Truth, it reappears at various times through the ages. This is well reviewed in the book quoted by Churton. In previous centuries each manifestation has suffered the same fate as the first Gnostic Church. It is only in our more tolerant times (or a time when the Christian Churches have less power) that it can show itself.

It is against this background that we can return to the question of whether the Gospel of Thomas is rightly to be regarded as a Gnostic text. The eminent authority Professor Guilles Quispel * is emphatic in asserting that this is not a Gnostic text. Moreover, he maintains that it does not contain evidence of the wording having been changed to suit ideas that may have been current in the Gnostic Church or the Nag Hammâdi monastery. Such modifications, which are common in early texts, may take several different forms. Sometimes a phrase or word that is unacceptable is deleted, filtered out; this can alter in a subtle manner the whole tone of a text. Another form, which has a more significant effect, is to change a word to another with a related but different meaning; in particular, this can affect the implications of what remains. A third form is a straightforward addition.

Professor Quispel, however, goes on to consider the matter from a different point of view from any of the foregoing. This approach is based on identifying particular phrases and comparing them with other documents. These relate to three themes. The first is the creation of the physical world. The Gnostics rejected the idea that the creation of the world was by God, and it is common in their writings to see this reflected. It nowhere occurs in the Gospel of Thomas; in fact the contrary is the case, as in logion 77—'Cleave the

---

* In conversation with the author.

wood, I am there; lift up the stone, and you shall find me there.' The second relates to the bodily incarnation of God in Jesus. The Gnostics considered that it was an image of God, not the incarnation, that was manifested in the human Jesus. The Gospel of Thomas contains the saying 'I stood up in the midst of the world and I manifested to them in the flesh' (logion 27). This, Professor Quispel maintains, is characteristically non-Gnostic.

The third example relates to a passage in the Oxyrhyncus Greek version of the Gospel of Thomas which reads 'There is nothing buried that will not rise again', referring to resurrection of the body. This is a concept that Gnostics rejected. The emphasis on this passage is coupled to the view that the Oxyrhyncus version, which is generally considered to be dated at about 200 A.D., is nearer to the source than the Coptic version. If this is so, the Gospel of Thomas itself can be regarded as non-Gnostic, and the deletion of this passage from the Coptic edition may be due to the Gnostic Church. There is, however, another way of looking at this, based on the view—held by some scholars—that the Oxyrhyncus version is a later redaction than that which was translated into Coptic. In this case, that passage might have been added to make this Gospel nearer to those of the Canon, especially John's.

Professor Quispel comes to his conclusion based on such specific points. Exactly the same result is obtained by considering the question within its overall background. When that is done, there seems to be no question that the Gospel of Thomas, while certainly an apocryphal Gospel, cannot be regarded as a Gnostic Gospel.

Coloration in the Gospel of Thomas

It is generally held that the Gospel of Thomas was composed in its present form not later than 140 A.D. in the Syrian city of Edessa. It was compounded from several sources, the main one being a collection of sayings of Jesus derived from the primitive group of his followers in Palestine; at that time these may have been in oral or, more likely, written form.

There is the influential view that it does not contain elements derived from the Gnostic Churches, and there do not appear to be any well founded suggestions that it was subsequently subjected to significant alteration by the time of the manuscript we now have, except for the translation into Coptic which gives every appearance of having been done skilfully.

So the question arises what type and degree of coloration might have been imposed on the primary collection of sayings of Jesus?

There is clear evidence that there was coloration derived from a Syrian encratitic movement of that time and place. Encratitism was an extreme form of asceticism. 'Encratitic ideas were not indigenous in Edessa, but were imported there from Alexandria' writes Professor Quispel. *

Asceticism was, and still is, an element of Christianity (and other religions for that matter), where it often takes the form of turning away from worldly pleasures, from material things, from their distractions—a turning to a simple life-style, to be

---

* *Gnosis and the New Sayings of Jesus*, 1969, in *Gnostic Studies* vol. II, page 201.

free to realize uncontaminated spiritual truths. It can lead to living a solitary life, or within a closed community. The archetypes of monastic life were those who went out to live in the deserts of the middle east.

When this came through to Syria, a sexual component was added to it (or perhaps this was amplified) such that the encratites may be called 'sexual teetotalers' (Quispel's phrase) or total abstainers from sexuality. This led to a rejection of any form of sexual activity, to the concept that the ideal form of the spiritual life was reserved for those who had accepted perpetual chastity, to the idea that distinctions between men and women were abhorrent, that procreation and birth were evil, and therefore that everything to do with the human body was a corruption. Our awareness, through the insights of the great twentieth century psychologists, of the power of the sexual instinct and the consequences of its repression, make it easy enough to see how all these fit together.

The evidence for the influence of this aspect of encratitic ideas on our version of the Gospel of Thomas lies in a few logia that denigrate the body, for example 56, 80, 105 and possibly 75, 87, 112. These however do not interest the present author sufficiently to warrant including any of them in this set of essays—most of us are accustomed to jumping over parts of the Bible.

Although it is impossible to know for certain, there is no evidence to suggest that the person composing the Gospel of Thomas invented anything; rather, he may have made deletions or altered words to affect the meaning. Two instances may be discussed, one minor and the other more significant.

First, an early writer renders the same tradition as in logion 16 as –

> For there will be five in a house,
> three will be against two,

and two against three,
the father against the son,
the mother against the daughter,
the mother-in-law against the daughter-in-law.

This is very near to its version in Matthew and Luke (*10:34,35; 12:52,53*). But in our version the feminine element has been replaced by the masculine alone. This, Professor Quispel maintains, is characteristically encratitic.

More important is the use of the word MONAχOς in the Gospel of Thomas. This Greek word occurs typically in encratitic writings, ★ and it does not appear earlier than about 140 A.D.—in fact it is a key element to cause scholars to attribute that date to this Gospel. There it has the meaning of a bachelor, a consecrated celibate, one who has renounced the world, and become a wanderer without home. Further, a monachos owes his name to the union of his heart with the divine and to the complete union of his being; he has become the complete man. When applied to women, it confirmed virginity, and through its spiritual quality gave a status that was higher than the norm for that time. Scholars certainly consider that this is the meaning that the composer of the Gospel of Thomas meant to give to it wherever it occurs. But this may have been an instance where a redactor takes a word in the original, in this case the Syraic *iḥidaja*, and invests it with his own meaning. However, we have a colloquial term 'loner' which may well be nearer to the original intent. This important word occurs in logia 16, 49 and 75. In every case it becomes appropriate to convey the sense of persons whose quest for spiritual Truth has necessitated going out on their own, becoming independent of even those near to them, and standing on their own feet. Then they may find the oneness they seek.

★ A Guillaumont, *Aux Origines du Monachisme Chrétien*, Spiritualité Orientale No 30, 1979

Such considerations enable us to 'decolorize' our version of
the Gospel of Thomas, to remove the only coloration of
significance.   Then, instead of this logion being about a clash
between generations, the younger accepting the new teaching
which their parents cannot, it becomes a prompt to take us
beyond the ties and the encumbrances even of the family so
that, by standing independently, we may find the oneness
which lies beyond.

    Jesus said:

    Perhaps men think

    that I have come to cast peace upon the world,

    and they do not realize

    that I have come to cast divisions on the earth,

    fire, sword, conflict.

    For there will be five in a house,

    three will be against two,

    and two against three,

    the father against the son,

    and the son against the father,

    and they shall stand up, being 'loners'.

New lights from the Gospel of Thomas

Spiritual Truth may be likened to a great jewel—the greatest there is—with many facets. Over the millenia great souls have discerned it, perhaps to a greater or lesser degree, and some have sought to help others share what they have found. In doing this certain aspects of that Truth are presented, each dealing with one facet of the jewel.

What distinguishes a cut diamond from the pale pebble found in the ground is that light may enter any one of the facets and, being reflected around within, emerges as a sparkling ray. So it is, as a great soul presents a facet of Truth for the earnest seeker. In all traditions 'light' symbolizes spiritual Truth, and its entry within illumines the individual.

The special value of the Gospel of Thomas is that it presents many new lights. These may be regarded in either of two ways. In the first, new light is thrown on some of the teachings of Jesus, elements we did not have before from the scriptures. In the second, facets of Truth that have been presented by other great souls are now to be seen presented also by Jesus.

One of the key themes of the Gospel is to know who or what one is at one's very centre. This use of the word 'to know' is of a very fundamental type as when we say "I know that I am myself and no-one else". The following passage from logion 3 gives this emphasis –

When you know yourselves
then you will be known,
and you will be aware that you are
the sons of the Living Father.

Here is an assertion of the union of the individual being with the divine, the essence of the mystical experience. Surely it is the objective of the spiritual search.

This knowing at one's centre is quite different from believing or having faith in something—of being believers or one of the faithful. Being known inwardly and by the individual it has great conviction or certainty, and this is entirely independent of any external influence or of the mediation of any ecclesiastical authority.

This attainment of deep knowledge is to release us from a particular condition. There is no hint in this Gospel of the Fall of Man or that it is from sin that we are to be saved. Instead, the Master is quite specific that it is from poverty that spiritual Truth is to release us, as where that logion goes on to say –

But if you do not know yourselves

then you are in poverty,

and you are the poverty.

This condition of spiritual impoverishment—or darkness or drunkenness as it is sometimes called—which the Master is seeking to eliminate by all he is giving, is referred to again in logion 29 where he says –

But I, I marvel at this:

about this great wealth

put in this poverty.

This inner knowledge is to be attained by turning to the Master to receive what he has to offer –

Know Him who is before your face,

and what is hidden from you shall be revealed to you:

for there is nothing hidden that shall not be manifest.

(Logion 5)

It is a knowledge that resolves the fundamental questions of living and gives a certainty and richness, whereupon a mutual indwelling will be established –

Jesus said:

He who drinks from my mouth

shall become like me;

and I myself will become him,

and the hidden things shall be manifest to him.

(Logion 108)

This attainment of inner certainty is also referred to in many sayings as the Kingdom or the Kingdom of heaven. But this is no remote place. Again from logion 3 –

But the Kingdom is at your centre

and is about you.

Furthermore in this Gospel neither is the Kingdom remote in time—at the millennium or to be found after death—but it is to be known during our earthly life. Thus in logion 51 –

His disciples said to him:

On which day will the repose of the dead come about?

And on which day will the new world come?

He said to them:

What you expect has come

but you, you recognize it not.

and in logion 113 –

His disciples said to him:

On which day will the Kingdom come?

Jesus said: It will not come by expectation.

They will not say: "Behold, it is here!"

or "Behold, there!"

But the Kingdom of the Father is spread out over the earth

and men do not see it.

The attainment of the Kingdom—a state of being that is in the here and now—is accompanied by a repose; this is akin to the peace and harmony that comes from being sure about oneself inwardly. In logion 50 –

If they question you

"What is the sign of your Father in you?"

say to them: "It is a movement with a repose."

In logion 60 the Master's hearers are urged –

You yourselves, seek after a Place for yourselves

within Repose . . .

And in logion 90 –

Jesus said;

Come to me,

for easy is my yoke

and my lordship is gentle,

and you shall find repose your yourselves.

This Gospel throws new light on the symbolic light itself –

There is light at the the centre of a man of light,

and he illumines the whole world.

If he does not shine,

there is darkness.   *(Logion 24)*

And again in logion 50 in answer to another question "Where were you from?", his disciples are told to say: –

"We came from the light

there, where the light was,

[shining] by itself."

Then we are given most emphatically –

Jesus said:

I am the light that is above them all.

I am the All.   *(Logion 77)*

That is very characteristic of this Gospel—to express some of the most significant sayings in the fewest of words.

The Gospel of Thomas follows the common practice that where 'he or she' is intended it says 'he', or for 'man or woman' it says 'man'. Also it uses 'Father' as we usually do in the Lord's

Prayer. On the other hand, it gives examples of the spiritual sensitivity and discernment of women as disciples, for example Salome recognizes the spiritual quality of the Master and proclaims "I myself am your disciple" *(logion 61)* just as did the woman at Jacob's well *(John 4:19, 29)*; and it likens the Kingdom to a woman who hid leaven in the dough *(logion 96)*.

However the Gospel throws new light on the spiritual equivalence of men and women. Thus instead of the exclusively masculine form of the diety we have *(logion 105)* –

He who knows the Father and the Mother . . .

and the striking logion 101 –

. . . for my mother has begotten me

but my true Mother gave me Life.

These show that Jesus was in tune with a widespread attitude of his time; it got lost during the following centuries, and people struggle nowadays to recover it.

The final logion of the Gospel has to be considered with practical common sense. In the first place it is said to a group of disciples including men accustomed to a male-dominated world, Peter being their spokesman. Further, we have to consider the implications of the retort and assertion of the Master: it is unworthy to imagine the Master saying he will merely make women ape men. It is also inadequate to imagine that he has in mind that men have some superior quality and that he is going to raise women to that level. Rather, we have to accept that he is giving an assurance that for true spirituality we each need to reach a single level of oneness that is higher than womanhood or manhood. This assertion by a Master, written in a document from antiquity, can alone give a proper basis for the trend we see developing in various ways in the religious life of our own times –

Simon Peter said to them:

Let Mary go out from amongst us,

because women are not worthy of the Life.
Jesus said:
Behold, I will guide her being,
in order that I make her as a male
that she also shall become a living spirit,
who resembles you males.
For every woman who makes herself as a male
shall enter the Kingdom of the heavens.

Realistic Situations in the Gospel of Thomas

A major difference between the Gospels of the Bible and the Gospel of Thomas is that the former not only give a great deal of narrative but also set the scene in which many of the teachings of Jesus were presented. Also, they show the reactions of his disciples and other listeners, this being one of their especially illuminating qualities. By comparison, the Gospel of Thomas does only little of this. It does not attempt to do so, for essentially it is a collection of sayings. In this respect it may be likened to the hypothetical collection of sayings that scholars call 'Q' and consider to have been used by Matthew and Luke in making their Gospels, building on the earlier one of Mark. (But note that many of the sayings in 'Q' and in the Gospel of Thomas are very different.)

Nevertheless, the Gospel of Thomas sets many of its sayings within realistic situations, and even for some the outward situation is essential for the meaning. To bring this out, it is possible to group them together. In the first place there are responses to disciples or those standing around. In the simplest examples we have reactions to ordinary people: 'A man said to him: Tell my brothers to divide my father's possessions with me. . . .' (*logion 72*); or 'They said to him: Tell us who you are so that we may believe in you. . . .' (*logion 91*). Logion 79 is another such. Here out of a simple statement, Jesus can present something of value.

More significant is when the disciples question him. 'Show us the Place where you are, because it is necessary for us to

seek after it. . . .' *(logion 24)*; '. . . Shall we then, being
children, enter the Kingdom? . . .' *(logion 22)*. In each Jesus
can give directly a response that reveals a facet of his teaching.
Perhaps more interesting is when they assert one of their
preconceptions. Then he has to correct their thinking. 'Tell
us in what way our end will be.' *(logion 18)*. Instead of
speaking about death, he asks 'Have you therefore discerned
the beginning in order that you seek after the end?' and takes
them into a life of happiness independent not only of death
and birth but also of time itself. Again a kindred question:
'On which day will the repose of the dead come about? And
on which day will the new world come? . . . What you expect
has come but you, you recognize it not.' *(logion 51)*. Here the
disciples, not mere bystanders, came with ideas of the
resurrection of the dead and of the coming of the day of
judgement. He said it was in the here and now, but only their
own blindness prevented them seeing it. For us, this raises
the whole question whether the emphasis on these topics in the
Canonical Gospels was from Jesus or added by the later writers.

The two logia after that are also correcting preconceptions.
But it is Peter, who we all love so much, who is really rebuked
in logion 114: 'Let Mary go out from amongst us, because
women are not worthy of the Life. . . . I will guide her being
. . . that she also shall become a living spirit who resembles
you males. . . .' As this is developed in the logion a great
spiritual truth is unfolded, one that sets the true relationship
between men and women, and exposes the weakness of so
much in modern feminism.

There are other examples of a named disciple playing a key
rôle. Mary, in logion 21, asks 'Who do your disciples
resemble?' and the response starts off by likening them to
small children, and goes on to present in a pictorial form a deep
truth. Salome has one of the finest parts; in logion 61 she
starts by questioning 'Who are you, man? Is it even as he

from the One that you reclined on my couch and ate at my table?' From his response, she instantly gives herself as a disciple, and then there is unfolded one of the most profound truths about the surrendering * of the ego in order to become filled with light.

Another way of looking at the realistic situations concerns the stories themselves. Very many of the logia are presented in the form of an actual happening, an outward story with an inner meaning that is deeper. This is the essence of a parable. The use of parables was one of Jesus' great means for conveying spiritual truth. He was one of the first teachers to use this method, and it is generally considered to be a hallmark of the genuineness of the recorded words.

Several of these are familiar to us from the Bible. Thus there is the story of the wise fisherman (*logion 8*), the sower and the seed (*logion 9*), the guests being called to the dinner (*logion 64*), the heir of the vineyard (*logion 65*), Caesar's coin (*logion 100*), the shepherd seeking the lost sheep (*logion 107*) and finding in the field the hidden treasure (*logion 109*). However, it is very well worthwhile comparing the versions in the Gospel of Thomas with those in the Biblical Gospels. There are always differences. Sometimes these are of the type that could result from variations in recounting the sayings in an oral tradition, and are of little consequence. More often there is a brevity and directness in the forms within the Gospel of Thomas. This is one of the guiding lines that scholars use when considering authenticity or originality. It is the case that as a saying is developed, in being passed from one person to another or in progressing from a verbal form to a written form, additions or glosses are made, usually with the intent of clarifying the meaning. There are examples of this in the *Presentation* of the Gospel of Thomas itself: if one compares

---

* In the Coptic the word used may mean 'a desert' or 'empty'.

the basic text given in manuscript with any of the Paraphrases, it will be seen that the latter very often add words.

What is more important is that sometimes the differences go beyond this. Consider as an example the first of those logia. In Matthew's Gospel *(13:47)* it is an impersonal net that is thrown into the sea, rather than a fisherman at work. Professor Gilles Quispel * makes clear that other early sources including Clement of Alexandria used this distinctive feature. Furthermore, he shows that the form of this saying is much closer to Aramaic speech than that in Matthew's Gospel. He writes 'Thomas speaks about man and his wisdom. He has the god-sent luck to find the one great fish, the Kingdom of God. He decides to cast away everything else, because this one thing is the only thing that is valuable. It is the same as that of the parable of the pearl.' And when we turn from the words of the saying to its context, we find that Matthew has a substantial addition, with essential words leading up to it, giving an allegorical interpretation. At the close of the age, the angels will come out and separate the evil from the righteous, and throw them into the fire where men will weep and gnash their teeth. This is the eschatology in the future, the last judgement, whereas the Gospel of Thomas presents a realized eschatology, a fulfilment in the here and now. Professor Quispel writes –

> 'The real issue is whether [this] leads us back to a stage of tradition before the Gospels and enables us to establish that Jesus preached a realized eschatology. The present author has reasons to suppose that this question should be answered in the affirmative.
>
>   The Kingdom of the Father is spread out
>   over the earth
>   and men do not see it.   *(Logion 113)*'

* *Tatian and the Gospel of Thomas*, 1975, Brill, pages 104 –107.

Logion 13 presents a realistic situation for which we need to piece together what is to be found in Mark's Gospel (*8:27 –30* expanded in the other synoptic Gospels), the Gospel of Thomas and what can be seen by going today to Israel. The river Jordan has always assumed a special significance for the Hebrew people, in part for its history and in part because it continues to flow throughout the year, unlike the wadis that dry up. Its source is not merely water oozing up from the ground, but a true bubbling spring gushing out from a cave in the rocks into a pool. Just as pilgrims today go in their thousands to the source of the Ganges, so in early days a visit to the source of the Jordan in the land of the Phillipians was an act of devotion. So much so that Herod Philip embellished the nearby city for them but by naming it after the Roman Caesar he angered the Jews. Today many shrines and monuments surround that pool, and no doubt it was so in the earliest years.

Soon after the start of his ministry, Jesus having gathered his first disciples from around the Lake of Galillee, it might come as no surprise if he had suggested a visit to the source of the Jordan, some seventy kilometres to the north. Arriving there, we are told he asked 'Who do men say I am?' This must have been early, before men had recognized his rôle. In the Canonical Gospels it is given to Peter to identify him as the Messiah—or the Christ as written in our Bible. However, in the Gospel of Thomas the picture is presented of Peter likening him to a righteous angel, and Matthew being perhaps influenced by the shrines dedicated to the wise men and philosophers. The text shows Thomas being overawed by the majesty he discerns. This discernment Jesus recognizes as a true inner awakening '. . . Because you have drunk, you have become drunk from the bubbling spring which I have made to gush out.' Whereupon he took Thomas aside, and spoke to him alone. It is widely testified that a spiritual Master can discern the potential of a follower, and pass on the higher truths only when there is the readiness to receive them. We are not told what was said, apart from there being three sayings. Some suggest that these were the three words rendered as 'Thou that art' or 'I am that I am'; but the Coptic and Greek require the meaning of three logia.

It is the sequel that is significant. On his return, the others question Thomas who responds –

>   If I tell you one of the logia that he said to me,
>
>   you will take up stones and throw them against me;
>
>   and fire will come forth from the stones and burn you up.

Thomas recognized (or had been warned) that that logion was a blasphemy; he could also see that it had a consuming fire within it. Jesus had to tell him something that must have been truly daunting for a Jew turning to be a Christian. Let us remember that Jesus went to his crucifixion also for a blasphemy. Now, how could that record of a realistic situation possibly have been made by anyone other than him to whom it occurred? What would be the point of anyone else recording it or inventing it? It is the signature by Thomas to his Gospel.

But it does not end there. Mark's Gospel is often regarded as the record of Peter's teaching, from which stemmed the Churches of the west. Was there some sleight of hand, or wishful thinking, that attributed this first recognition of Jesus' quality to Peter? And even moreso. The Gospel of Thomas was quite widely known at the time of the consolidation of the Canon. Rather than argue about logion 13, might it not have been more effective to belittle Thomas by making him doubt Jesus on his appearance to the disciples? Scholars know that episode to be a later addition to John's Gospel—but all too often ordinary people refer to 'doubting Thomas'. When a footballer cannot play the ball, he may play the man.

Symbolism in the Gospel of Thomas

The Gospel of Thomas deals with spiritual Truth at a very high level. It is the case that almost everything in it is symbolic. That is not to say that its meaning is obtuse or concealed or made difficult; rather it is that ordinary words and phrases do not have the capacity to convey what it has to say, and so of a necessity it has to use symbolism. Symbols have a power to convey meaning beyond bare words.

Let us start with a very simple example of symbolism. In logion 32 we can read –

A city built upon a high mountain and made strong,
cannot fall, nor can it be hidden.

This saying is attributed to Jesus. He cannot possibly have been giving guidance to burghers where to plan their new town, nor advising their military men. He must have been addressing ordinary men and women and encouraging them to find a higher, inner spiritual strength. Not only would this carry them through adversity, but it would also serve as an example and encouragement to others.

We are familiar with a saying like logion 34 –

If a blind man guides the being of a blind man,
both of them fall to the bottom of a pit.

It is obviously referring to a spiritual blindness. But there is an added quality in the phrase 'to guide the being'. This is not merely to advise or to instruct. Nor is it just to take his hand. The being of a person symbolizes something very deep within him, and for that to be guided there is needed a very special quality, probably compounded of love and dedication.

Likewise there is added intensity in the phrase 'the bottom of a pit'. False guidance at that level can be calamitous.

The word 'light' is widely used symbolically in spiritual teachings to indicate the richness that comes from the awareness of spiritual Truth, with its warmth and glow. And it is often contrasted by 'darkness'. It comes several times in the Gospel of Thomas, as in logion 24 –

> His disciples said: Show us the Place where you are,
>
> because it is necessary for us to seek after it.
>
> He said to them: He who has ears let him hear;
>
> There is light at the centre of a man of light,
>
> and he illumines the whole world.
>
> If he does not shine, there is darkness.

We have two sayings that refer to repose. Part of logion 50, advice being given to the disciples –

> . . . If they question you:
>
> "What is the sign of the Father in you?"
>
> say to them:
>
> "It is a movement with a repose."

and logion 90 –

> Jesus said:
>
> Come to me;
>
> for easy is my yoke and my lordship is gentle,
>
> and you shall find repose for yourselves.

This is very definitely a symbolic repose, not merely a resting. It is a vibrant state, with everything inwardly alive, but in an equipoise through being totally in harmony.

Logion 8 has several symbolic elements –

> The Man is like a wise fisherman
>
> who cast his net into the sea;
>
> He drew it up from the sea full of small fish.
>
> Amongst them, he found a large and good fish.

That wise fisherman, he cast all the small fish
          down to the bottom of the sea,
he chose the large fish without trouble.
He who has ears to hear let him hear!

The Man—rendered here with a capital letter—is of course one who is wise enough to find spiritual Truth. The story of the fisherman choosing between the large and the small fish is a symbolic representation of discrimination coupled with our capacity for the exercise of free will. And it also says that a single source of true spiritual insight is to be preferred to a multitude of minor sources.

A motif on the cover and title page of this book, and also of the *Presentation* from which the quotations of logia are taken, is entirely symbolic. The cross signifies a gospel from an early Christian Church. Rather than the usual shape to signify that on which Jesus was crucified, it takes account of very strong traditions that in 52 A.D. the apostle Thomas went on to set up a Church on the Malabar Coast of south-west India, which still exists. Together with a sister-Church they are both linked to Antioch and its precursor Edessa, one of the four great centres of early Christendom. This Church, like the Coptic Church of Egypt, uses a cross with equal arms; furthermore, it graces its crosses with lotus buds about to blossom, a flower that carries great symbolic meanings to those peoples.

This symbolically living cross is set within a circle, the whole forming a mandala. In many ancient wisdoms a mandala symbolizes wholeness or Oneness—one of the key themes of the Gospel—and it has been taken up in modern psychology where is it referred to as individuation, the process of coming to an inner unity and harmony.

Comparisons with the Biblical Gospels

Often one of the first questions asked about the Gospel of Thomas is how it compares with the Gospels of the Bible. Indeed, most of the books and articles published on this Gospel deal with this topic, and many of them do so to the exclusion of anything else.

It seems that the motive is related to the authenticity of this Gospel. That must be based on an assumption that the Biblical Gospels, with all their tradition and the study given to them, are the basis for reference. However it overlooks the possibility that the sayings of Jesus might have been more comprehensive than those recorded by the evangelists—three of whom had never met him. Putting this another way, instead of relying on the synoptic idea of similarities between the various Gospels, which might be the result of the work of redactors, there might be value in differences that come from the words of Jesus.

It is the case that over seventy of the logia, or parts of them, are related to passages in the Biblical Gospels. Phillipe de Suarez has identified a relevant set of texts, and arranged and published them (in French) in *L'Évangile Selon Thomas*, 1975 version, where they occupy 97 closely printed pages even without any commentary or notes. The cross-references to these are given in an Annex to this essay. Glancing at that, it may be noted that the order or structure of the sayings differs widely between the various Gospels, and often only a part of a logion in this Gospel is equivalent to a passage elsewhere. In an attempt to aid the reader who wishes to embark on this study, a scheme of stars has been here used to suggest those comparisons of most significance; of course this can only be arbitrary.

The outcome of the studies that have been made may be said to fall under two headings—the general and the particular. To begin with, the Gospel of Thomas is of a different genre from the others. It contains hardly any narrative, it does not recount events in the life of Jesus, it tells us very little of the reaction and response of others to Jesus, whether followers or those hostile. It confines itself to being a collection of sayings. In this respect it may perhaps be likened to the hypothetical source document 'Q' used by Matthew and Luke. Therefore, and this is to be emphasized, it can in no way displace the other Gospels, but only supplement them.

At a deeper level, the Gospel of Thomas does not refer to belief or faith; it does not describe any miracles; there is no attribution of greatness to God, nor of his acting in judgement; neither does Jesus have any judgmental rôle nor forgive sins; Jesus makes no claim to be Son of God or even Son of Man; there is no mention of the passion of Jesus and the resurrection of Christ; to use long words, it is free of millennial or apocalyptic concepts, of future eschatology or a Last Judgement, of a contrast between Heaven and Hell; fear nowhere enters in. Of course it could be said that thereby the Gospel is gravely emasculated, but on all such themes something different, and yet of significance, is written. For anyone not indelibly committed to those doctrines, it offers alternatives coming directly from the Master.

For particular comparisons, certain examples may be taken. In logion 34 –

> If a blind man guides the being of a blind man,
> both of them fall to the bottom of a pit.

The 'being' of a person is an advanced concept, and the guiding of his being is an idea worthy of Jesus. The 'blind guide' of Matthew 15:14 can be seen as a simplification (perhaps it was the more subtle saying that Peter did not grasp); such popularization is typical of many of the different renderings in the Biblical Gospels from what must have been originally the same sayings. Very often the form in the Bible appears to have been simplified no doubt with the intention that it may be acceptable to the members of the catholic—meaning universal—Church; whereas the form in the Gospel of Thomas is more difficult. This difficulty however often stems from the sayings using the language of parables, which has the capacity to reach to levels of awareness that are not only deep but also dependent on the capability of the hearer (see essay *Parables*).

Logion 8 gives a distinctive version of the parable of catching the fish –

> The Man is like a wise fisherman
>
> who cast his net into the sea;
>
> he drew it up from the sea full of small fish.
>
> Amongst them, he found a large and good fish.
>
> That wise fisherman, he cast all the small fish
>
>   down to the bottom of the sea,
>
> he chose the large fish without trouble.

Whereas Matthew *(13:47–50)* starts with a net that is thrown in the sea, Thomas refers to Man in his deepest understanding who is likened to a wise fisherman, and it is he who carries out the action. Finding the large and the small fish is common to both versions. But the important point is made that not only does the wise fisherman have the discrimination to identify and choose the large and good fish, but that through this discrimination he can do it without trouble. Here then is a guide to wise living, and it is different in a fundamental way from the theme added in Matthew where the kingdom of heaven is likened to the angels separating evil persons from the righteous, and all to await the close of the age when there will be fire, weeping and gnashing of teeth.

The story about Caesar's coin *(logion 100)* appears at first similar to the versions to which we are accustomed –

> They showed Jesus a gold coin
> and said to him:
> Caesar's agents demand taxes from us.
> He said to them:
> Give the things of Caesar to Caesar,
> and the things of God to God,
> and that which is mine, give to me.

Thomas did not give the background of the episode, he might have thought it ephemeral. But he did add that last line. Now, one of the features of several of the sayings in this Gospel is their hierarchical sequence, which builds up a cumulative effect. The startling point is that God is not at the summit, but what we can give to Jesus—in devotion and loyalty—makes the difference to our lives. No-one but a Master could have dared claim that.

When Matthew gives the story of finding the hidden treasure *(13:44)*, it is found by chance in a field belonging to someone else, and is then covered up. It appeals to our simple emotions of avarice, elation and deception—all from the ego. Thomas is very different –

> The Kingdom is like a man
> who owned in his field a hidden treasure
> it being unknown to him.
> And after he died, he bequeathed it to his son.
> The son not knowing it,
> took that field and sold it.
> And he who bought it came.
> While he was ploughing, he found the treasure;
> he began to lend money at interest
> to whoever he wished.   *(Logion 109)*

Here the Kingdom is likened to a man and what is within him, even though he neither knew it himself at any time during his life, nor helped his son to find it. It is only found by one who worked to discover it, always latent within himself. Here we have the same theme as the Hymn of the Pearl (essay *The Church that Treasured*), a teaching of the highest or deepest spirituality. Then a question we might ask ourselves is whether Jesus gave two stories about a hidden treasure, one simplistic and the other profound; or whether by the time Matthew's Gospel was passed on to us changes had been made, for certainly the concept in Thomas leaves no place for a mediating priesthood and would divest them of their power.

By the time the saying of logion 68 was established in the beatitudes of the Bible (*Matthew 5:11, Luke 6:22*) Christians were suffering persecution. Therefore it is very understandable that a phrase 'Happy are you when you are disliked and you are pursued', using a word previously applied to the pursuit of animals, could be adapted to bring comfort— 'Blessed are you when men revile and persecute you'. In the saying of the next logion 69 –

Happy are they who have been pursued in their heart.

It is they who have known the Father in truth.

this interpretation is not possible, it becomes necessary to accept that to be pursued in the heart, to have the urge to find spiritual Truth at the depth of one's being, is the way to happiness.

So it might be possible to go on—and there are hundreds of instances of other comparisons in the literature on the Gospel of Thomas. It can be seen that much in this Gospel may have originated in the same or similar sayings as passages in the other Gospels, but reasons for the differences are not entirely clear. A strange thing then seems to occur. In most fields of work, as one goes deeper some increasing order may be found, summaries made, conclusions reached. But that is not the case with these comparisons.

This forces us to look in another direction. We know that the Gospel of Thomas or its precursor existed during the formative period of the Gospels of the Bible, and was used within a Church that was quite widespread. We also know that much in it, and teachings derived from it, were anathema to those in other Churches that were gradually establishing orthodoxy and coming to ascendancy. Those Churches were forming themselves on the transmitted traditions and the primitive scriptures, and at the same time establishing the accepted form of those scriptures. Might it have been possible that the Gospels of the Bible were consciously moulded so that similarities with the Gospel of Thomas did not occur?

To look for something which by its very nature is not visible is quite peculiarly difficult. It is something we have to do with computers. When we write a program of instructions to carry out some task, we always have to check against residual mistakes—program 'bugs' we call them. And we have to allow for the possibility that despite all our searching some bug will remain, which some day will bob up and cause, for example, the auto-pilot to crash a jumbo jet with all its souls on board. The technique we use is to approach the problem from some entirely different direction, which may reveal a clue to the trouble.

There may be a clue to our strange situation. Dr. John A T Robinson towards the end of his life of scholarship argues persuasively for the priority of John's Gospel. It is not so much, he maintains, a matter of dates, but more its spiritual primacy and an authority that comes from one who knew Jesus alive—which is more than we can be sure of for any of the other evangelists.

Robinson comments – *

* John A T Robinson, *The Priority of John*, SCM Press, 1985, page 327. He lists the words in Greek, here rendered into our alphabet and each followed by its major dictionary translations.

"There is little doubt that John's Gospel was seized upon by the Gnostics . . . as 'their' Gospel. . . . John seems to have been well aware of this danger, of being so near and yet so far, in the words he apparently quite consciously avoids. . . . He seems to wish to give his opponents no handle by using [the following words]"

pistis :	faith; an assenting unto, belief, trust, confidence
sophia :	wisdom, skill, knowledge, learning
gnosis :	knowledge, discernment, wisdom
physis :	nature, the principle which produces all things
pneumaticos :	pertaining to the breath or wind; spiritual, divine, perfect
mysthrion :	a mystery, moral truth veiled under an external representation, moral import of a parable; doctrine of the gospel
apokalyphis :	a discovery, revelation or unfolding
plhroma :	a supplement, fulfilment, completion
eikon :	an image, statue, representation

We will instantly recognize that all these great words relate to concepts that are crucial to spiritual Truth—and yet John's Gospel as we have it does without them (at least in the Greek). That is very strange; surely we should look a little further.

These concepts are central to the Gospel of Thomas. Although the only valid ancient copy we have was done over into the Coptic language as best they could, five out of those nine words are even used in it in Greek and perhaps three others in their Coptic equivalents, only the apocalypse being unmentioned.

So there is a possibility that there may be rather more to the observation by Robinson than meets the eye. Perhaps the 'opponents' he refers to were not only the Gnostics but also these other followers of the teachings in the Gospel of Thomas.

However, there is a much more significant possibility. All the Gospels of the Bible were undergoing changes during the early centuries, being harmonized to each other and to the Churches' teachings. We know that John's Gospel had a difficult time, extending over several centuries, before it was accepted into the canon. In this process did some of those Church worthies deliberately remove these words from John's Gospel? But perhaps not quite skilfully enough, so that someone with Robinson's ability could spot that this had been done 'quite consciously'? Might John, like Thomas, have written his Gospel using these great spiritual words, taken directly from Jesus?

Annex

Cross–references to equivalent passages
in books of the New Testament

Logion	Matthew	Mark	Luke	John	Other	Significance
3.7			17:21			★★★
4.3–5	11:25–26		10:21			★
.7–8	19:30	10:31	13:30			★
5.3–4		4:22	8:17			★★
		10:26	12:2			★★
8	13:47–50 Particularly the absence of the addendum used by Matthew					★★★
9	13:1–9	4:1–9	8:4–8			
	13:18–23	4:13–20	8:11–15			★★★
10			12:49–50			★
13.4–5	16:13–20	8:27–30	9:18–21			★★★★
.23–26	19:40					★
14.8–13	10:11–14	6:10–11	10:5–11			★
.13–16	15:11	7:15				★
16	10:34–36		12:51–53			★★
17	13:14–17		10:23–24		1 Cor 2:9	★
18	16:28	9:1	9:27 This may not be a valid equivalent			★
20	13:31–32	4:30–32	13:18–19			★★
21.2–4	11:16–17		7:31–32			★
.13–20	12:39–40	24:43–44				★★
22.1–4	19:13–14	10:13–15	18:15–17			★
	18:3	10:15				
.13	19:4–6	10:6–9				★★★
24.6–9	6:22–23		11:34–36	12:36		★★★
25	22:34–40	12:28–34	10:25–28			★
	7:3–5		6:41–42			★
26						
31	13:57–58	6:4–5	4:24			★
32.2–5	5:14					★
.3–4	7:24–27	6:47–49				★
33.1–4	10:27		12:3			★
.5–6	5:15–16		11:33			
	4:21		8:16			★★
34	15:14		6:39			★★★
35	12:29	3:27				★★
38	-		17:22			★
39.2–6	23:13		11:52–54			★★
.7–8	10:16		10:3			★
41	13:12		19:26			
	25:29					
	4:25		8:18			★
44		12:31–32	3:28–30	12:10		★★
45	7:15–20		6:43–45	12:33–37		★★
46	11:11	7:28–30				★★

Logion	Matthew	Mark	Luke	John	Other	Significance
47.1–8	6:24	16:13				★★★
.9–19	9:16–17	2:21–22	5:36–39			★★★
			Addition at Luke 5:39 inverts the meaning			
48.2–3	18:19					★★★
.4–5	17:20		(17:6)			
	21:21	11:22–23				
53					Rom 2:25,29	★
54	5:3		6:20			★★
55	10:37–38	14:26–27				★★
	16:24–25	8:34–35	9:23–24			
57	13:24–30					★★
	13:36–43					
58	5:10					★★
	10:39		17:35	12:25		
	16:25–26	8:35–37	9:24–25			
61.2–3	24:40–41		17:34–35			★
62.4–6	6:3–4					★
63			12:16–21			★★
64	22:1–10		14:15–24			★★
65	21:33–41	12:1–9	20:9–16			★★
66	21:42–43	12:10–11	20:17–18			★
68	5:11		6:22			★★★
69.6–7	5:6		6:21			★
72			12:13–15			★
73	9:37–38		10:2			★
76.2–7	13:45–46					★★
.8–12	6:19–21		12:33–34			
78	11:7–10		7:24–27			★★
79.1–6			11:27–28			★
.7–9			23:29			
86	8:19–20		9:57–58			★★★
			Prof. Quispel attaches special importance to this			
89	23:25		11:37–40			★
90	11:28–30					★
91	16:1–3					★
93	7:6					★
96	13:33		13:20–21			★
99	12:46–50	3:31–35	8:19–20			★
100	22:15–22	12:13–17	20:20–26			★★★
104	9:14–15	2:18–20	5:333–35			★★
107	18:12–14		15:3–7			★
108.2–4			6:53	but may be out of context ★		
109	13:44					★★★★
113			17:20–21			★★
114	19:12		This may not be a valid equivalent ★★★			

A Scrap

A scrap, a tiny thing. When any mother, and almost every father nowadays, looks on their new-born baby, she or he sees something perfect. This may perhaps be the first time perfection has been consciously seen. Not only the whole, lying there, but every detail, right down to those tiny nails on the fingers and toes, made just right. The hands will clasp round one's finger. Forgetting that this is an instinct from our monkey forebears, when the baby had to hang on tight because the mother used her fore-arms for walking in the trees, our love is transmuted into the feeling that the baby is expressing its love—through the most elementary of our five senses, touch.

At that moment, for that mother and father, the perpetration by Paul of the doctrine of inherent original sin may appear as a monstrous lie. She or he knows, at the inmost core of the heart, that their baby is pure, purity itself, and born of love. And then his other inventions may also fall into question, that Jesus came as the saviour from our sinfulness, his passion and crucifixion a sacrifice to cleanse all mankind and the world of sin and suffering, and that bliss can only be known in the paradise of heaven after our death. So perhaps from that moment fundamentals of the edifice of the established Christian Churches may crumble. What is so amazing—even more so, a wonder—is that the inherent urge within each one of us for the spiritual still leads us into the Churches.

Jesus said:

The man old in days will not hesitate
to ask a little child of seven days

> about the Place of Life,
> and he will live, for many who are first shall become last
> and they shall be a single One.   *(Logion 4)*

There are some who cannot face this. Some translators of this Gospel make it 'a man old in years' asking a 'little child of seven', giving the impression of the old man sitting before Jesus as a child prodigy. But the Coptic will not allow this. It is entirely clear : the same word is used for the days of the child and the days of the man. The four evangelists could not accept it; neither could Paul nor any of the Church Fathers. It is nowhere in the Bible or the Church teachings. Jesus here is speaking directly to the mother and the father, they are seeing in their baby the One indwelling spirit—not only the Place of Life but the ultimate Place of their lives.

But look again at it. Using just one's ordinary reasoning it must be surely one of the greatest of nonsenses. How possibly could anyone of maturity learn from an infant ? It is necessary to get inside it. And the way in is through an awareness of the ego. A baby is born without an ego. To look on the baby may perhaps be the first time that egolessness has been seen. That is its perfection. Jesus was without ego, he was perfect. It is a way of defining the meaning of perfection. Each of us started that way, and all too soon we start—we have to start—to build up our ego, and gradually it becomes strengthened. When in our last maturity we can get back to our first egolessness, then we shall become a single One, a harmonious whole.

> Know Him who is before your face,
> and what is hidden from you shall be revealed to you :
> for there is nothing hidden that will not be manifest.
>
> *(Logion 5)*

Just a scrap, tiny but showing us perfect Oneness.

On Seeking and Finding

What turns a Seeker into a Finder ? What makes a person a Seeker in the first place ? What does being a Finder mean ? What benefits result from being a Finder ?

A person becomes a Seeker by having the urge to seek after spiritual Truth—it is as simple as that. In logion 69 we can read –

> Happy are they who have been pursued in their heart.
>
> It is they who have known the Father in truth.

To be pursued in the heart here means to be utterly filled, in a deep unquenchable way, with the urge to attain to spiritual Truth. Notice that this logion comes well on in the Gospel, and a grasp of the main themes will show that it is not the urge itself that gives the happiness but the consequences of having that urge.

So what follows on the urge to be a Seeker ? Jump right back to the very start of the Gospel (*logion 2*) –

> Let him who seeks not cease from seeking
> until he finds;
> and when he finds, he will be turned around;
> and when he is turned around, he will marvel,
> and he shall reign over the All.

Here in a masterpiece of brevity—so concise that it is difficult immediately to grasp the whole import—are most of the answers to our questions. Taking it more slowly, the continuation of the urge will result in become a Finder. Done in the right way, this is something that just happens.

There is the plain assurance of logion 92 –

Seek and you will find.

reiterated by logion 94 –

He who seeks shall find,

and to him who knocks it shall be opened.

In the finding, however, 'he will be turned around'. This is a rendering of a word that also carries the meanings of to be disturbed, or to be troubled as when a pool of still water is stirred about. It involves the casting off of an outer shell, a coming to know one's inner Self—which is always there, right from the start, but veiled. It is summarized most intensely in the extraordinary logion 42 –

Become your true selves, as your egos pass away.

This could be rendered 'Become yourselves, passing away', with the meaning that the hold of the material, the body and the ideas of the mind is relinquished. It comes to the same thing. *

In coming to his true Self, most assuredly 'he will marvel'. And why, and what at ? In logion 3 –

But the Kingdom is at your centre

and is about you.

When you know yourselves

then you will be known,

and you will be aware that you are

the sons of the Living Father.

The Kingdom in this Gospel is one of the terms that point towards what we might call spiritual Truth. It is something that is known at one's very centre—experience. So this logion says that to be a Finder is to be a Knower.

---

* The key word, Greek, ΠΑρΑΓω, is used elsewhere in the Bible for a wanderer or one who passes by, a mendicant or hermit. To use that here misses the inner meaning.

This finding, this coming to know one's Self, is helped
forward by coming close to the source –

Jesus said:

Know Him who is before your face,

and what is hidden from you shall be revealed to you:

for there is nothing hidden that shall not be manifest.

(Logion 5)

from which follows the great affirmations of the Master –

I will give you what no eye has seen,

and what no ear has heard,

and what no hand has touched,

and what has not arisen in the heart of man.

(Logion 17)

Come to me, for easy is my yoke and my lordship is
gentle,

and you shall find repose for yourselves.   *(Logion 90)*

Jesus said:

He who drinks from my mouth

shall become like me;

and I myself shall become him,

and the hidden things shall manifest to him.

(Logion 108)

Something New

Something new is an emphatic theme of the Gospel of Thomas. That is to say, in the words of Jesus as recorded in this Gospel, he was emphatic that what he was presenting was new.

This is a marked contrast with the general tenor of the books and epistles of the New Testament. In these the authors or redactors wished to emphasize the continuity of the New Testament with the Old. This came from a Hebrew concept of history, as having a linear or progressive quality which demonstrated the steady unfolding of God's plan for mankind, and of man's reward—when obedient—to that process. It was clearly a factor in the choice of those records to be included in the Canon.

It shows particularly in the final form of Matthew's Gospel, where there are many instances of events or sayings of Jesus that have been related to quotations from the Old Testament. There, something recorded in the Torah is taken to be a prophecy fulfilled by Jesus. This theme of the dependence and continuity of Christianity with the Hebrew religion is emphasized in the practice in the Church's liturgy of usually including a reading from the Old Testament followed by one from the New.

None of this can be found in the Gospel of Thomas. Instead, what we find are many sayings that mean, or at least imply, that Jesus was giving something that was not just an advance, development or progression of what was

before, but was a new departure for those who heard and saw
him.   It may be something new for us.

> I will give you what no eye has seen,
> and what no ear has heard,
> and what no hand has touched,
> and what has not arisen in the heart of man.   *(Logion 17)*

> His disciples said to him:
> Who are you that you should say these things to us?
> [Jesus said to them]: From what I say to you,
> are you not aware who I am?
> But you, you were even as the Jews:
> for they love the tree, they dislike its fruit;
> and they love the fruit, they dislike the tree.   *(Logion 43)*

> His disciples said to him:
> Twenty-four prophets spoke in Israel
> and they all spoke about your nature.
> He said to them:
> You have abandoned Him who is living before you,
> and you have spoken about the dead.   *(Logion 52)*

Logion 47 is the most telling on this theme, if only because
of the impact of the reiteration of very simple everyday
situations.   Seven word-pictures are presented here as a
coherent series, all emphasising the same point and building
up its impact.   In characteristic Semitic manner, Jesus drives
home his point as by the clanging of a tocsin.

> Jesus said:
> It is impossible for a man to mount two horses,
> for him to stretch two bows;
> and it is impossible for a servant to serve two masters,
> otherwise he will honour the one and offend the other.
> Let a man drink old wine

and now he longs to drink new wine.

And new wine is not poured into old wineskins,
lest they should burst;

and old wine is not poured into a new wineskin,
lest this be spoiled.

An old patch is not sewn onto a new garment,
because there would be a mismatch.

Then, Jesus was speaking to people who came chiefly from
two backgrounds. There were the Jews of the countryside,
committed to their lineage but not too happy about the nit-
picking emphasis on minute details of the Law and its daily
observance; and those from a simple form of Greek culture
that had lost its true impulse and become bogged down in a
world of demi-gods and spirits who inhabited everything and
directed every action, leaving no space for the free will of
man. The other Gospels tell of two occasions when he spoke
to the four- or the five-thousand. What he gave them was
sustenance, so 'all were satisfied'. Perhaps inaudible to some
of them, they could see him with both their outer eyes and
their inner eye. With that, they saw something new, and it
was satisfying.

Today, the words of Jesus can speak freshly to those of us
who come from either of two backgrounds. There may be
some who are not happy with the offerings of the established
Churches, who cannot go along with the inventions of Paul and
their development in the doctrines of the Church Fathers, who
no longer wish to share in a love-feast that perhaps is seen as
transformed into a vicarious participation in a human sacrifice.
There are others who are not satisfied by the multitude of sects,
all the -isms, TV-evangelists or pseudo-psychological teachings
on offer. We cannot see him with our outer eyes. Let the
memories of his pitiable, pitiful broken body on the cross be
put on one side. Get a copy, the best that can be obtained,

of his radiant living form portrayed in an icon of the Eastern Orthodox Church. Let this be put in some special place of your home. Let living flowers be always kept beside it. Spend some minutes of every day before it, gazing intently. Then the inner eye may come to see him. There will be something new, and it too will be satisfying.

The Kingdom is like . . . .

The term 'Kingdom' occurs frequently in the Gospel of Thomas. Sometimes it is with other words—the Kingdom of the Father, the Kingdom of heaven, for example. But most often it is on its own, and these are the most significant instances.

What is important is not the word itself but the concept it is referring to. Scholars consider that this word is the Hebrew way of referring to the concept. The Greek way of referring to it uses the words the One or the All; they are used in this Gospel also, always carrying great significance. It is possible that Jesus used the Hebrew form and also the Greek form, depending on the group of people he was addressing at any particular moment, and both have been faithfully recorded in the Gospel. In our contemporary terminology the terms Ultimate Reality, or the Ultimate, or the Reality, might be used. When spoken, emphasis is always placed on these words in a sentence, and when written the capital letter has to be used.

The first thing for us to do is to release ourselves from the assumption that it means the Kingdom of Heaven, something that is elsewhere and comes down to us or is only to be known in another life. For anyone accustomed to the Bible or the Christian Churches this may be difficult, but the effort needs to be made if what this Gospel has to offer about the Kingdom is to be received.

In the Gospel of Thomas the Kingdom is in the here and now, potentially available to every one of us, and in this life.

The sayings are quite specific about it. Logion 82 puts this
negatively (note the tenses).–

> He who is near to me is near to the fire,
> and he who is far from me is far from the Kingdom.

Other logia express it positively –

> If those who guide your being say to you:
> "Behold the Kingdom is in the heaven,"
> then the birds of the sky will precede you;
> if they say to you: "It is in the sea",
> then the fish will precede you.
> But the Kingdom is at your centre
> and is about you.   (*Part of logion 3*)

> His disciples said to him:
> On which day will the Kingdom come?
> Jesus said: It will not come by expectation.
> They will not say: "Behold, it is here!"
> or "Behold, there!"
> But the Kingdom of the Father is spread out over the earth
> and men do not see it.   (*Logion 113*)

We cannot assume that we are all that much better than
those around Jesus in those days. So perhaps there is a very
real chance that we do not see it either.

Jesus was wanting to refer to the greatest thing there is.
Which word was to be chosen for his Hebrew hearers? They
lived in a community that had developed only to a certain
extent from a tribal state. All around them were kingdoms,
some ruled over by what we would call petty-kings. Being
within a kingdom, within the realm of the king, gave them a
degree of peace, security, justice and prosperity that was not
possible otherwise. Their whole well-being depended on it.
Added to that was the sense of grandeur, majesty and mystique
that they felt to be associated with the king himself, the

quintessence of the kingdom. It could appeal to their emotions of wonder, loyalty and gratitude. All in all, there was nothing greater in their ordinary lives, nothing more splendid or wonderful that they could visualize. Kingdom was a good word to choose; we need to see its significance in their eyes.

This splendour, however, was not a worldly spendour. It is of a different nature, to be conveyed by very homely similies.–

The disciples said to Jesus:
Tell us, what is the Kingdom of the heavens like?
He said to them:
It is like a grain of mustard, smaller than all seeds;
but when it falls on the tilled earth,
it sends forth a large stem
and becomes a shelter for the birds of the sky.

(Logion 20)*

The Kingdom is like a shepherd
who owned a hundred sheep.
One among them, which was the largest, went astray;
he left the ninety-nine,
he sought after the one until he found it.
When he had toiled, he said to the sheep:
I desire you more than the ninety-nine !   *(Logion 107)*

The Kingdom of the Father is like a man, a merchant,
who owned merchandise, and found a pearl.
That merchant was wise:
he sold the merchandise,
he bought this single pearl for himself.

---

* At that time people thought of three heavens, superimposed like domes above the flat earth. This has no significance in the Gospel of Thomas.

You also, seek after treasure which does not perish,
which remains in the place
where no moth comes near to devour,
and no worm destroys.   *(Logion 76)*

The Kingdom is like a man
who owned in his field a hidden treasure
it being unknown to him.
And after he died, he bequeathed it to his son.
The son not knowing it, took that field and sold it.
And he who bought it, came.
While he was ploughing, he found the treasure;
he began to lend money at interest
to whoever he wished.   *(Logion 109)*

The Kingdom is not a place, but a condition of being;
something that is, and is experienced as a radiant stillness.   It
is to be found, and entered, and known.

If you abstain not from the world,
you will not find the Kingdom.   *(Part of logion 27)*

Happy are the 'loners' and the chosen
for you shall find the Kingdom.   *(Part of logion 49)*

These children who are being suckled are like
those who enter the Kingdom. . . .
When you make the two One, . . .
then shall you enter the Kingdom.   *(From logion 22)*

He who amongst you becomes as a child
shall know the Kingdom,   *(From logion 46)*

Those here who do the wish of my Father . . .
These are they
who shall enter the Kingdom of my Father.

(From logion 99)

Now, it is one thing to hear this of the Kingdom. However, the Gospel of Thomas goes on to tell of how we may find, enter and know it, this is one of its very special qualities. Many of the logia refer to ways to follow to reach it, they are guides, not from one who defines the Kingdom but one who is given to helping others to find it. These have to be told symbolically, by presenting word-pictures, which we may use. Several occur in a set of logia built round the phrase 'the Kingdom of the Father is like . . .' –

The Kingdom of the Father is like a woman
who was carrying a jar full of flour
while walking on a long road;
the handle of the jar broke,
the flour streamed out behind her on the road.
As she did not know it, she could not be troubled by it.
When she had reached her house
she put the jar on the ground;
she found it empty.   *(Logion 97)*

The Kingdom of the Father is like a man
who wishes to kill a giant.
He drew the sword in his house,
he struck it through the wall
in order to be assured that his hand would be confident.
Then he slew the giant.   *(Logion 98)*

The Kingdom of the Father is like a woman,
who took a little leaven,
hid it in dough and of it made large loaves.
He who has ears let him hear!   *(Logion 96)*

The means of finding the Kingdom lie in overcoming the dominance of the ego. In the first, the woman was so absorbed by contemplation of the Kingdom that her ego was lost, even though she was unaware of its going and could not be troubled. By contrast, in the second the man wished to extinguish his ego. He summoned his inner strength, tried it out to be sure this would suffice, and slew his ego. In the third we are shown that this overcoming of the little self, done inwardly, blossoms into the greatness of the Kingdom.

Let us turn again to logion 22, in its entirety. This is one of the great logia of this Gospel. It brings together the Hebrew and the Greek ways of referring to the concept, and gives a plenitude of insights into the need to rise above the duality of the ego and the real Self; in doing so, the spiritual replaces the temporal.

> Jesus saw children who were being suckled.
> He said to his disciples:
> These children who are being suckled are like
> those who enter the Kingdom.
> They said to him:
> Shall we then, being children, enter the Kingdom?
> Jesus said to them:
> When you make the two One,
> and you make the inner even as the outer
> and the outer even as the inner,
> and the above even as the below,
> so that you will make the male and the female
>   into a single One,
> in order that the male is not made male
> nor the female made female;
> when you make an eye in place of the eyes,
> and a hand in place of a hand,
> and a foot in place of a foot,

and an image in place of an image,
then shall you enter the Kingdom.

The term 'Kingdom' also occurs in logia 21, 54 and 114.

Parables in the Gospel of Thomas

Maurice Nicoll has written very helpfully on the nature and significance of parables * –

> 'A parable is a medium of connection between a lower and a higher meaning. In ancient teaching, Man is taken as a link between a higher and a lower world. Man lives physically on earth by the light of the sun but psychologically he lives by the light received by his level of understanding, a far more wonderful light. A language exists that connects Man on the level of earth with man on the level of 'heaven'. *It is in this language that parables are cast.* It is a specific language speaking, in terms of earthly objects, of meanings represented at a higher level—of things belonging to the understanding. . . .
>
> 'If a man were fully awake he would see the objective meaning of all things around him. It would be enough if he were fully awake in the *emotional centre*—that is if he was conscious in the Higher Emotional Centre. The language of the Higher Emotional Centre is the language of the parable. It is a language of vision. . . .
>
> 'If a man were awake there, through its illumination he would see the significance of all things. *He would see things as they really are.* He would pass from a world of physical things into a world of supernatural, inconceivable meaning. He would be in a state of *objective consciousness.*

★ *The Mark*, Robinson & Watkins, London, 1954, shortened from pages 58–60, 143.

'Every word in a parable in the Gospels has a special
meaning, belonging to this language that connects
visible things of the world with the understanding of the
mind at the Higher Emotional Centre. A parable is
alive as it has connection with higher levels, and
conducts force from higher levels and so has life in it.

'A parable conducts permanent or eternal meaning,
and will be understood by everyone according to his
level of being. That is, it will grow in meaning as a man
grows in his level of understanding. . . .

'A great part of the real teaching given by Jesus about
man and his possible evolution is contained in the
parables. They are designed to fall upon the internal
understanding from which alone a man can grow, for a
man is his understanding. So it can be said that a
parable is to make a man think; and unless a man
begins to think in a certain way for himself, metanoia is
impossible and so his evolution cannot begin. For this
reason Jesus emphasized that metanoia is the first
essential step.'

In a very real sense therefore everything in the Gospel of
Thomas is of the nature of parable, as announced in the very
opening statements –

These are the hidden logia . . .

He who finds the inner meaning of these logia . . .

Let him who seeks not cease from seeking

until he finds

. . . and he will marvel.

However, in this essay only the longer passages are considered,
those which almost take the form of stories.

We have in this Gospel the familiar parables of the Sower
and the Seed, and of the Fisherman. The first of these is fully
considered by Maurice Nicoll * where attention is given both

★ *Op. cit.* pages 60–81.

to the words of the parable and to explanations of it given by
Jesus as recorded in the other Gospels. Two things are to be
noted. The Gospel of Thomas does not give the explanations.
Secondly, some of the words or phrases in the explanations are
somewhat removed, even alien, from those of the parable
itself—such as 'the evil one comes and snatches away what is
sown in his heart' (*Matthew 13:19*), 'that they might not believe
and be saved' (*Luke 8:12*), 'tribulation and persecution arises on
account of the word' (*Matthew 13:21*), the thorns as 'cares and
riches and pleasures of life' (*Luke 8:14*) instead of our emotions
that veil spiritual Truth. The reader may wish to consider
whether the explanations have the significance of the parable
itself, and perhaps go on to ask himself whether it was Jesus who
added these words that diminish meaning, or the evangelists or
later redactors. Perhaps Jesus, and certainly Thomas, considered that it was more effective for the recipient himself to work
out the inner meanings. Here is Thomas' unadorned version –

Behold, the sower went out.
He filled his hand, he threw.
Some seeds indeed fell on the road;
the birds came, they plundered them.
Others fell on the rock
and did not take root in the earth
nor did they send up their heads to the sky.
And others fell on thorn trees;
these choked the seeds
and the worm ate them.
And others fell on good earth;
it brought forth good produce to the sky;
it bore sixty per measure
and one hundred and twenty per measure.   (*Logion 9*)

The minimum of words, the touch of the Master, speaking this
language of parables.

As for the parable of the Fisherman, we have already seen (essay *Comparisons*) that the Gospel of Thomas makes him a wise fisherman who can thereby discern the One Truth for his present life, without the future escatological explanation added in Matthew's Gospel with its foretaste of Hell, all so utterly different from everything in this Gospel.

The parable of the lost sheep as we are given it in logion 107 is entirely clear and unambiguous –

> The Kingdom is like a shepherd
> who owned a hundred sheep.
> One of them, the largest, went astray;
> he left the ninety-nine,
> he sought after the one
> until he found it.
> When he had toiled,
> he said to the sheep:
> I desire you more than the ninety-nine !

The One is likened to a single sheep, the largest, sought after and, when found after some toil, the most desired. The Kingdom is likened to this. The sheep only 'goes astray', it is not a lost soul for whom the shepherd sets up a party of rejoicing; nor is there any confusion about heaven with a sinner or ninety-nine righteous persons—surely additions by Luke (*15:4–7*).

Logion 64 gives us the parable of the guests being invited to a dinner but each one excusing himself. Note the very simple scenario—each one of the excuses has to do with material or worldly concerns, paying off a trader, completing a house purchase, arranging a feast even for a marriage, collecting the farm rent. No wonder there is the conclusion that those who base their priorities on materialism—the abiding preoccupation of western society towards the end of the twentieth century—shall not enter the Place of my Father.

Surely in something so grave, and so timely, there is no need for any more diffuse or convoluted explanations.

Likewise logion 65 gives the parable of the Heir to the Vineyard, which we know to be the picture Jesus presented of the manner in which the religious leaders of his time were to react to, reject, seize and crucify him. It is immediately followed by the saying of his being the corner stone that was rejected. There are other logia in which Jesus comments on the lack of acceptance to which he was subjected. We recognize or interpret these when they occur in the Biblical Gospels as presaging his Passion. So it may be of significance that Thomas includes them, but does not go on to make any mention of the Passion nor of a subsequent resurrection.

It may be noted that in the synoptic Gospels those two separate parables are mixed up, and in addition are jumbled with threats of divine retribution.

Logion 60 has no equivalent in the other Gospels –

They saw a Samaritan,

carrying a lamb, going into Judea.

He said to his disciples:

Why does this man carry the lamb around?

They said to him:

In order that he may kill it and eat it.

He said to them:

As long as it is alive he will not eat it,

but only if he kills it and it becomes a corpse.

They said:

Otherwise he will not be able to do it.

He said to them:

You yourselves, seek after a Place for yourselves within Repose,

lest you become corpses and be eaten.

It is not an easy parable (which may in part be due to difficulties in translation) and that might account for its exclusion. Nevertheless, it is presenting a contrast between the lamb that is alive and the fate that befalls it when killed. So, he tells the disciples, they are to seek a Place within Repose—and the sign of the Father within is a movement with a repose *(logion 50)*—lest they are to be extinguished.

Nor is there anything like logion 28 –

Jesus said:

I stood up in the midst of the world

and I manifested to them in the flesh.

I found them all drunk;

I found none of them athirst,

and my heart was afflicted for the sons of men

because they are blind in their heart

and they do not see

that empty they came into the world

and that empty they seek to go out of it again,

except that now they are drunk.

When they shake off their wine,

then they will change their knowing.

In the *Presentation* the phrase 'to change one's knowing' is used to render the Greek word metanoia, noted by Maurice Nicoll as the first essential step to spiritual evolution. In the Gospel of Thomas it has an even more emphatic meaning, for it links directly to its key word ϹΟⲅⲱN—a profound certainly known at the depth of one's being. ★ Further, in this Gospel the word 'empty' is linked to the absence of ego, as happened to Salome in logion 61 (essay *Unacceptability of the Gospel*), to

★ The *Presentation*, Note 6 to logion 3.

the woman in logion 97 who carried a leaking jar of flour, and as in our beginning and end of logion 18 (essay *Death and resurrection*). So our blindness, our drunkenness, inhibits our spiritual evolution, and afflicts the heart of Jesus.

The parables of logia 21 and 37 (the former quite difficult) share an idea in phrases 'They strip off their outward façade before them', and 'When you strip yourselves of your shame' in the other. There is a clue in both that little children are also referred to. In logia 4 and 18 we have already learnt that what they are free from is the ego. This may be likened to the persona of an actor in any Greek play, a mask held up of stereotyped design that announced to every member of the audience the particular rôle; an idea taken into Jung's psychology as the outward form that each of us learns to adopt to guard the inner psyche. The simile continues in the second of those logia, where garments as might be used by an actor are to be discarded. These three parables give a foretaste of one of the most important elements in the Gospel of Thomas and in the teaching of its early Church—the overcoming of the dominance of the ego. A later essay, *Release from the Ego*, is given entirely to this.

The teaching of Paul
and the teaching of Jesus

One of the consequences of the discovery of the Gospel of
Thomas is to make more clear the distinctions, even the
differences, between certain aspects of the teaching of Paul and
the teaching of Jesus. Many people have written and spoken
on this. Often the comparisons are made from general
considerations, or from references to early literature of the
Christian religion. However it needs to be born in mind that
such literature is itself largely a product of the orthodox
established Church, which depended so much on the teachings
of Paul. That is not to say that anything otherwise had been
ruthlessly suppressed, although that certainly might have
happened; but for documents to survive through many
centuries it is necessary for people to treasure them, otherwise
they merely deteriorate and become lost. Now, with the
discovery of the Gospel of Thomas, we have a source for
comparison that escaped both the purging and the decay.

The clue for this essay came from the monumental volume
by Professor W H C Frend *The Rise of Christianity*. ★ In his
chapter on the personality and mission of Paul, he writes –

'Only with reservations can Paul be called the inter-
preter of the religion of Jesus.' *(page 92)* and

'Paul's opponents from Palestine, intent on preserving
the word wherever it might be spread within the bounds

★ Darton, Longman and Todd, London, 1984.

of Judaism, had some justification for their attempts to refute the 'Pauline heresy'. ' *(page 104)*

With respect to the second, the use here of the word 'heresy' is no doubt meant to be with its later meaning of 'something wrong', rather than its early meaning of 'distinctive' (see essay *A heretical Gospel*). Also one needs to take into account that Frend had earlier explained that in the very early decades many followers of Jesus had seen their way forward in terms of a development of the established Jewish religion which nevertheless had to maintain its purity.

However, one also needs to take into account with both these quotations that Frend's purpose was to explain the rise of the established Church and that, in a very fundamental way, he is deeply committed to it. Therefore to be able to express these views signifies an honesty that enhances their significance.

Although Frend does not do so, we might start with Paul's teaching on original sin, an inherent sinfulness in every person, because it touches everyone at his or her beginning. Not only that—in some centuries it has assumed a greater rôle than it does now. In the seventeenth century it was proclaimed so intensely that George Fox, founder of the Quakers, coined the phrase that the clergy "preach up sin to the grave", one could not get away from it until death; and one only has to look at mediæval wall paintings in our churches to imagine, behind the faded paint, the horrors of hell awaiting the sinners.

In the Gospel of Thomas Jesus is saying –

> These children who are being suckled are like those who enter the Kingdom. *(Logion 22)*

> He who amongst you becomes as a child shall know the Kingdom. *(Logion 46)*

> "We came from the light

there, where the light was, by itself. . . .
We are His sons
and we are the chosen of the Living Father."

(Logion 50)

The images are manifest to man
and the light that is amongst them is hidden.
In the image of the light of the Father
the light will reveal itself
and his image is hidden by his light.   *(Logion 83)*

In the days you see your resemblance, you rejoice.
But when you see your images
that in the beginning were with you,
which neither die nor are manifest,
oh! how will you bear the revelation !   *(Logion 84)*

It is not merely the innocence of childhood. He proclaims
that each of us comes from the light; this light is both the
image of the Father and also the primæval image in each man
or woman; it was in the beginning both of the Ultimate and
also of each of us, and the seeing of the wonder of it may be
almost too much for us to bear.

Paul placed much emphasis on belief. He was in good
company. The Hebrew religion was, and is, based on belief
in its one God; the Greek religions in their panoply of gods.
Apostles preached in terms of belief, at least that is how they
are presented in our scriptures. In the magnificent Church of
which Paul may rightly be regarded as the founder, belief is
the keystone of the arch over all, it is the key to the lock, to
the door, to the way, to salvation, to the Life. In every form
of the Creed, the believer asserts his beliefs.

In the Gospel of Thomas only the disciples refer to belief—
and then only once *(logion 91)*. It never occurs in the words

of Jesus. Instead, again and again he uses the word 'to know'. This kind of knowing is different from knowledge *of* something, which is of the mind. Knowing, rightly, is the assimilation in one's inmost being of experience. It is something in its own right, without qualification or without the addition that the knowing is *about* something.

> Happy are they
> who have who have been pursued in their heart.
> It is they who have known the Father in Truth.
>
> *(Logion 69)*

> You scrutinize the face of the heaven and the earth,
> and him who is before you
> you have not known . . .   *(Logion 91)*

Paul teaches that Christ is the Saviour. Only once in the Gospel of Thomas does the word 'to save' occur. Look how it does appear –

> When you bring forth that in yourselves,
> this which is yours will save you.   *(Logion 70)*

The saving is done by something that is ours, and in ourselves. It just has to be brought forth.

And for Paul it is sinfulness that Christ is saving us from. What is it here that we are to be released from? –

> . . . But if you do not know yourselves
> then you are in poverty,
> and you are the poverty.   *(Logion 3)*

> But I, I marvel at this:
> about this great wealth put in this poverty.   *(Logion 29)*

> If a blind man guides the being of a blind man,
> both of them fall to the bottom of a pit.   *(Logion 34)*

. . . but when he is divided
he will be filled with darkness.   *(Logion 61)*

. . . If he does not shine,
there is darkness.   *(Logion 24)*

It is from poverty—the lack of awareness of spiritual
Truth—and blindness to that Truth, and living in a darkness,
that we are to be saved from.

Paul taught that the supreme act of salvation was a sacrifice
on the Cross. For all those who suffer this stands as a leading
light, a source of comfort whose depth cannot be plumbed.
Jesus had seen suffering, in all its physical, mental and psychic
forms, in so many around him; he may well have wished to
give the great consolation.

Here the great gift is something different –

Look on him who is living
as long as you live . . .   *(Logion 59)*

Know him who is before your face,
and what is hidden from you shall be revealed to you,
for there is nothing hidden that shall not be manifest.
                                              (Logion 5)

I am the light that is above them all.
I am the All.
The All comes forth from me,
and the All reaches towards me.
Cleave the wood, I am there;
lift up the stone,
and you shall find me there.   *(Logion 77)*

He who drinks from my mouth shall become like me;
and I myself will become him,
and the hidden things shall manifest to him. *(Logion 108)*

Frend writes 'There was no question in [Paul's] mind of humanity possessing some saving and eternal spark of the Divinity that would preserve them from the world.' (page 98). Paul's teaching was of a risen Christ with whom, either at the Final Judgement or after our deaths, we might find a oneness through the atonement for our sins by that ultimate sacrifice. In the Gospel of Thomas the awareness of the Father or Oneness can be for the here and now –

> When you know yourselves
> then you will be known,
> and you will be aware that you are
> the sons of the Living Father.   (Logion 3)

> When you make the two One,
> you will become Sons of man,
> and if you say: "Mountain, move away,"
> it shall move.   (Logion 106)

> His disciples said to him:
> On which day will the Kingdom come?
> Jesus said: It will not come by expectation.
> They will not say: "Behold, it here!"
> or "Behold, it is there!"
> But the Kingdom of the Father is spread out
>   over the earth
> and men do not see it.   (Logion 113)

Release from the Ego

While the ego can be regarded in its own right, it becomes clearer as a contrast with the real Self. There seems no need to do other than first to repeat what has been written before *

To recognize what is meant by the ego requires fundamental considerations. Each man or woman comprises body, mind and emotions, and a Self over all. Ordinary language reflects this awareness; we say "my body", "my mind and thoughts", "my feelings and emotions". These phrases come entirely naturally to us; we know them to be valid without anyone having to convince us. The point is: who is it who can say "my"? It is the real Self.

The real Self, the true Self are synonyms. So too are reality, truth, the absolute, the ultimate; and also terms used in this Gospel—the All, One, Unity, the Kingdom, Life, the Living, the Father, Kingdom of the Father, the Father and the Mother, light, the Pure Spirit, Kingdom of the heavens—all these are as facets on the jewel that is this. The jewel itself is of course beyond the capability of any word or words to describe—parts of something cannot describe the whole.

The ego derives from the mind, the emotions, the body and outward material factors. Being egoistic or selfish, self-opinionated, self-assertive or competitive, possessive, proud, changeable or vacillating, distressed

---

* Adapted from the introduction to the Paraphrases of the *Presentation*; it was written while in a special place.

or sad, despairing or fearful, thinking up concepts or doctrines, are manifestations of the ego. Suffering belongs to the ego.

Happiness and bliss, peace and repose and tranquillity, certainty and stability and assurance and steadiness, contentment, consideration and generosity, love and beauty, reliance, strength and fearlessness, knowledge, belong to the real Self.

We each naturally have, or grow to have, an ego. It is far more difficult to see it in oneself than in others— one of its tricks. It is the equation of oneself with one's body and mind. Due to the influence of the bodily senses and of the intellect and emotions, it readily becomes dominant. But as the centre of attention is transferred from the ego to the real Self so Truth becomes known.

This transference, in essence, consists in overcoming the dominance of the ego. This is best done by first recognising and accepting the ego, and then concentrating on the positive. If the attention is concentrated on the ego itself, this will merely be strengthened.

It is a mistake to think that this rejection of the ego involves a denigration of worldly activities and interests. No, this release from its dominance is to be distinguished from regarding the body, the mind and emotions, and the outer world as corrupt or sinful. It is entirely possible to admire the highest edifices of the intellect and of science, to wonder at the working of all the parts of the body, to be entranced by artistic or natural things, to treasure all the good things of daily life, and yet to stand one stage removed from them. Seen thus, at their highest these reach up toward the ultimate.

One of the great difficulties, one of the characteristics of the ego, is that it is extremely difficult to see within oneself. In fact, it is not apparent until it has been made apparent by someone else who is more free from it.   Likewise, when we have begun to see it, even within ourselves, it can creep back all unawares, and we really need the presence of someone who has less of it to make it again apparent to us.   The ego can be thought of as being everything that Jesus had not got.

The thing to do is first to come to see it in others.   That gives a chance to recognize it.   As a start, look out for it on the television.   It is very extraordinary, but what makes a good 'television personality', what makes one so appealing to us, is to a considerable extent manifestations of the ego.   The plain egotism, the brashness, the assertiveness—there may even be bombast—are all clues.   Politicians now cultivate their television manners.   The quest for power and the cultivation of popularity come equally from the ego.   Talk about catching two birds in one net!

Apart from the small-ads, advertisements appeal to the ego, exclusively.   As we see the natural breaks—however contrived —the strident pages in the glossy journals, the hoardings, by identifying what it is they are directed to we can become aware of something of the ego within ourselves.   It is certainly a serious matter that television, which can bring so much of good right into our homes, is being allowed or even encouraged to have the content of its programmes determined by those who manipulate and foster this appeal.   Nevertheless, each of us may turn that round by making every instance help identify our own ego, so that it may be quenched.

The converse of this—the other side of the same coin—is to see the absence of ego in others.   Putting our memories to the 1980s, perhaps the instance most people could share would be when the Dalai Lama came into our homes on television.   Or we can visualize through our screens, behind the outward ceremony that is a necessity of his position as Pope, the inner freedom from the ego of Paul John II.   Mother Teresa must be without ego.   And in an earlier century James Naylor towards the end of his life took himself beyond the dominance of the ego, to leave his most beautiful and profound writings. But it is not only these great souls who achieve it. In many communities there are individuals who, to a greater or lesser extent, instance their absence of ego. It is more likely amongst women than men, and it only needs an eye watching for it to discern its absence.

In the Gospel of Thomas there are a considerable number of logia which in their inner meanings relate to the ego. This is one instance of where the complementary nature of the Gospel of Thomas—bringing things that the other Gospels omit—is so important. Without an awareness of this concept, some of these logia seem to be devoid of even an outer meaning, they are true puzzles. In order to gain this contribution of the Gospel, it is necessary to consider all these logia together. They can best be identified by scanning through the Paraphrases in the *Presentation* looking for the word 'ego'. As an example, consider logion 35 –

> It is not possible to enter the house of the strong man
> and take it by force unless he binds his hands;
> then he will plunder his house.

Jesus was not there to counsel thugs. Looking further, we might note that Matthew and Luke (*3:27; 12:29*) associate this saying, by inference, with an external force, Satan. However, 'house' in the Gospel of Thomas usually directs us to our inner being. So looking further still, we find he is cautioning us that there is a strong man there, which is exactly the form the ego takes, assertive, ruthless and intent on remaining in command. It is always a struggle to overcome the ego, which first has to be identified and restrained. Once that is done, *its* domain can readily be emptied.

In logion 103 there must be more than counsel about protecting one's property –

> Happy is the man who knows
> where and when the robbers will creep in;

so that he will arise and gather his strength
and prepare for action before they come.

'Robbers' in the Gospel of Thomas are the forces within
us that take away the splendour of the awareness of the
Kingdom. The ego is a veritable band of robbers, wily,
persevering and creeping out of the undergrowth from all
directions. They keep on coming back at us. To become
aware of the manifestations of this force, to become strong
through contemplation on the qualities and powers of the real
Self, makes it possible to prevent their entry into our lives
and thus leads to happiness.

The ego acts as a veil over the real Self. The essence of
this aspect of the teaching of the Gospel of Thomas is that
the removal of this veil spontaneously reveals the awareness
of spiritual Truth. Whatever may be the labour of identifying
and then quenching the dominance of the ego within, the
reward is to discern the Kingdom of the Father. Logion 58 –

Happy is the man who has toiled to lose the ego,

he has found the Life.

The usual teachings of the Christian Churches do not build
upon the concept of the ego nor, more particularly, that the
overcoming of its dominance permits spiritual Truth to reveal
itself. Of course many Christians through the centuries,
especially amongst the mystics, have come to this awareness and
experience, but it may be said they have done it without the
guidance or support of their scriptures. Thus, in the Christian
civilization it is left to others, especially poets and mystics, to
speak or write of it. This is not the case in other great religions,
where it may be an essential component. It may go under
different names, sometimes it is called the 'little self', in contrast
with the real Self –

'awhile, as wont may be,
self I did claim;
true Self I did not see,
but heard its name.

I, being self-confined,
Self did not merit,
till, leaving self behind,
did Self inherit.' *

It might be queried, quite properly, that the Gospel of
Thomas does not itself use the word 'ego' nor any synonym.
When the question was put directly to Professor Quispel,
whether the concept of the ego was known and used in spiritual
teachings of that time and place, he emphatically replied
"Yes". One possibility is that Jesus would not have needed
to speak the word—he directly manifested the total absence of
ego. But perhaps more likely is that the absence of ego is to
be experienced, not read about. This at once puts this essay
into doubt but, quite simply, it is a risk that is felt to be worth
taking, even if only one reader of this book in a thousand is
helped come to the significance of the ego and the real Self.
The implication of this situation is that in the Church where
the Gospel of Thomas was treasured, the transmission of the
concept of release from the ego, with its revelation of spiritual
Truth, was most probably effected by example rather than by
teaching. That is to say, aspirants gained what they sought
by being in the presence of one who had overcome the
dominance of his ego, rather than by exhortation or precept.

Perhaps we might go on to consider an aberration of the
concept of the ego. All too often spiritual and religious
movements have embarked on a denigration or rejection of the
body and emotions, and sometimes of all worldly things.
Certainly it is legitimate that any emphasis on the spiritual
tends to put material things at a lower level. As we have seen
(essay *Coloration*) the Church that treasured the Gospel of
Thomas got mixed up with an extreme encratitic movement.

---

* Jalal al Din Rumi (1207–1273), one of the greatest Persian Sufi poets, quoted
 in *Man's Religious Quest*, Unit 21, page 71, The Open University, 1978.

This may perhaps have been under the influence of the Gnostic Church, which was very widespread at the time and placed emphasis on the evil nature of the physical world. However, the mistake is due to a lack of proper discrimination, of failing to recognize necessary distinctions. There is a vital, though subtle, difference between the release from the *dominance* of the ego, and denigration of the mind and body. Certainly as we go forward with our newfound wish to care for our planet and all living things, we cannot afford to make that mistake.

Discrimination provides the means to avoid falling into any such traps. Using it, it becomes possible to identify the ego and to see it as the key to the lock. As the dominance of the ego is overcome—which certainly involves work, the toil of the shepherd, the ploughing for the treasure, the summoning of inner strength—so the bolt draws back. Once freed, the door swings open of itself—the innate quest for the spiritual in every man and woman sees to that. Then it is possible to step forward, leaving behind poverty, darkness, intoxication, to move into the realm of light in which there is only the One.

On death and resurrection

There is a certain strangeness that throughout the established Christian Church the subject of death and a possible life
thereafter looms so large.

The greatest and most moving music composed in the West
is for requiems. The most splendid liturgy and spectacles
within cathedrals are on occasions of the death of great men
and women—excepting only the ecstatic happiness of the
celebration of Easter Sunday in the Eastern Orthodox Church.
Our Christian-based civilization remembers anniversaries of a
person's death, rather than great moments in their life. Our
doctors go to any length to put off our deaths. In our Church
services prayers are given to see us safely through the night to
the day beyond. The Churches' doctrines lay great stress on,
and derive much of their substance from, this topic. Our
morality, our guides to right daily living, are coloured by
concepts about rewards in heaven or torments in hell. The
paintings on the walls of our ancient churches, such that
survive, portray emphatically that contrast. Above all, the
most fundamental teachings of the established Churches centre
on the crucifixion of Jesus, on his resurrection and the
continuing presence of the spirit Christ, with whom departed
souls may seek companionship. From these countless men
and women, especially the bereaved, derive consolation and
solace in their occasions of greatest distress.

But search in the Gospels of the Bible for a concerted
teaching by Jesus on death. Look up 'dead' and 'death' in
Cruden's concordance. There is the episode with Lazarus,

and references to the death of Jesus; other passages can certainly be related to a physical or psychic death, akin to blindness or darkness from which Jesus seeks to release people—this is a symbolism. The records show Jesus going about, discerning the needs of the people around him, and working to meet those needs. But there is no sign that death was a pressing problem to those people. There is nothing in those Gospels, coming directly from the living Jesus, to substantiate the extreme emphasis our Churches place on death and an after-life. That emphasis must have been derived from doctrines made not by him.

The Gospel of Thomas takes a different approach to this profound topic. It refers to the matter at two levels. In the first place, 'to die' and 'dead' occurs quite often. But this is always with the simple meaning or implication that the living quality has gone out of the person or thing. It is usually in making a contrast with life or living. There is a finality about it; there is certainly no suggestion that there is a continuation after, and there is no hint of a rising again in a different or higher form.

In the second place, the Gospel of Thomas does refer specifically to death as it affects an individual. It is not silent in giving guidance and help about this. In doing so, it reaches to a much higher level. In this Gospel the word death occurs in three logia in the same sense and phrase, repeated. Thus, in logion 1 –

> And he said:
> He who finds the inner meaning of these logia
> will not taste death.

and from logion 18 –

> . . . Happy is he who will stand up at the beginning,
> he shall know the end,
> and shall not taste death.

and from logion 19 –

. . . He who knows them
shall not taste death.

Here it is clear enough that this is a symbolic way of speaking. And in the Paraphrases of the *Presentation* it is rendered by turning it round to find the underlying significance –

. . . And will find the Life that is independent of
the death of the body.

This is a true Life, lived in this life.

However, in a manner that is very characteristic of this Gospel, this theme arises within the contexts of other logia. Let us take the whole of logion 18 –

The disciples said to Jesus:

Tell us in what way our end will be.

Jesus said:

Have you therefore discerned the beginning
in order that you seek after the end?

For in the place where the beginning is,
there will be the end.

Happy is he who will stand up at the beginning,
he shall know the end,
and shall not taste death.

Note first that nowhere in the other Gospels is there such a direct question about death. Jesus, as is his wont, does not answer it in the way the disciples (or ourselves) might expect. Instead, he urges them to come to an awareness of something greater, to discern the beginning. He gives them (and us) work to do.

So it becomes necessary to seek out elsewhere what he means by the beginning. The clue comes in the immediately following logion –

Jesus said:

Happy is he who already was
before he is. . . .

Continue seeking in logion 50 –

Jesus said:
If they say to you:
"Where were you from?"
say to them:
"We came from the light
there, where the light was,
by itself. . . . "
and in logion 49 –
Jesus said:
Happy are the 'loners' and the chosen
for you shall find the Kingdom.
Because you are from the heart of it,
you shall go there again.

The light and the Kingdom are synonyms, and so is Life. So
we are being directed to come to an awareness of spiritual Truth,
independent of time in the sense that it 'already was and is'; it is
where we came from—being of 'the heart of it'—and where we
shall go. He or she who comes to be aware of the oneness of the
beginning and the end, who lives in this life with an awareness of
the Kingdom, will find the true happiness in the end.

In this way fear and uncertainty may be replaced by the
prospect and assurance of happiness, of finding the Oneness.
Through the awareness of this the bereaved who are left may be
able to use their love—itself a manifestation of the Kingdom
within—to transmute their grief into happiness for the departed.

It is all confirmed in logion 4 –
Jesus said:
The man old in days will not hesitate
to ask a little child of seven days
about the Place of Life,
and he will live,
for many who are first shall become last
and they shall be a single One.

On being a 'Loner'

It is indeed fortunate that there is a colloquial word that seems precisely to refer to one of the important concepts of the Gospel of Thomas —a 'loner'. Strangely, we have no proper word that conveys the right idea.

The term probably came from American pioneering days, of one who went out on his own, "Go west, young man !". It implies foremost an independence, with perhaps something of an adventure about it. It is a willingness to follow what one sees to the right for oneself, if necessary to go it alone; it is the opposite of being gregarious, of thinking and doing what others do just for the sake of being in their company.

A man in his maturity shared with four younger companions the adventure of walking across the last great uninhabited area in Europe, in northern Norway where the nomadic Lapps follow their herds of reindeer but no-one, yes no-one, resides. It is the size of Wales, and every necessity for a fortnight has to be carried in a rucsac. The feint path, the 'Kungsladen', goes into this region, passes through it, and leads out to houses and transport on the other side. On all sides are glorious mountains, mounds of great age rounded by the elements, not jagged like the alps; the path weaves through the valleys between them. Being mid-summer, the sun shone all day, melting the snow and enabling myriads of alpine plants to burst into life and throw up their flowers—such profusion, such variety, such delicacy in their tiny complex shapes, such dazzling brilliance of colours. Stopping to photograph these, intoxicated by their magic he often dallied long, and fell behind his companions.   Then striding along in this beautiful world, truly a loner, he suddenly sensed in the majesty of the mountains, which were only known through his miniscule being, the oneness of God and man.

Later, he was helped to see that the majesty and the miniscule were only a superimposition on the reality of Oneness, or the oneness of Reality.

In the Gospel of Thomas the word 'loner'—in Greek MONAχOς—occurs in three logia, all of them needing an awareness of its teachings to discern the intention –

> Happy are the 'loners' and the chosen
> for you shall find the Kingdom.
> Because you are from the heart of it,
> you shall go there again.   *(Logion 49)*

> Perhaps men think
> that I have come to cast peace upon the world,
> and they do not realize
> that I have come to cast divisions upon the earth,
> fire, sword, strife.
> For there will be five in a house,
> three will be against two,
> and two against three,
> and father against the son,
> and the son against the father,
> and they shall stand up, being 'loners'.   *(Logion 16)*

> There are many standing at the door,
> but the 'loners' are they
> who shall enter the marriage place.   *(Logion 75)*

In the first place, notice that the first also uses 'chosen', and the second uses 'divisions'.   These refer to the same concept. In the Coptic, and also in the Bible, 'chosen' carries the sense of being separated rather than being favoured; and the word 'divisions' here carries the sense of a positive type of discrimination, to separate light from darkness for example. Those who are to find the Kingdom need to be able to distinguish worldly things from what Jesus was offering.

The second logion at first sight appears to be about the discord that can arise between the younger and older generations, even within a family—we are all too familiar with this nowadays. But the last line adds a more significant meaning that to accept the new truth Jesus was offering it may be necessary to stand as loners.

It turns out that the word MONAχOϛ comes mainly to our notice in the spiritual writings of ascetic sects of antiquity, especially of the extreme encratitic form. * There it carries the meaning of solitariness and also, in particular, a sexual overtone of virginity or batchelorhood. Together with this, the word may carry something of 'oneness', which equally relates to batchelorhood. In fact, the use of this word in this Gospel is a primary reason for ascribing the date of 140 to its final form (or as some would say to its assembly from other sources, or others would say its fabrication by some impostor, one who had never prostrated before his Master in gratitude). Some writers have seen this encratitic coloration in the second and third of the logia above, and this seems very plausible if the approach to the Gospel of Thomas is made from the viewpoint of these ascetic sects. On the other hand, the original sayings may have used this word with its meaning of 'loner', but the ascetic coloration was introduced by the sect active in Edessa at that time.

---

* A Guillaumont, *Monachisme et Éthique judéo-chrétienne*, Judéo-Christianisme, Paris, 1972.

So this Gospel recognizes that to be a loner may not be the way for everyone, it may involve the loneliness of going out on one's own, but it can be the way to spiritual consummation and—because in our origin we come from the Kingdom *(logia 18 and 19)*—our happiness will be in the experience of Oneness as we find our way there again.

Oneness

It is not difficult to see that the All and the One refer to the same thing—more strictly they both point to the same place; either of them has to be complete, and there can be only one completeness. What is more difficult is that the Kingdom is also the same. The former are Greek ways of referring to this, and the latter is the Hebrew way.

The Gospel of Thomas helps us towards this right near the beginning. In logion 2 –

Let him who seeks not cease from seeking
until he finds;
. . . and he shall reign over the All.

Then very soon after we have –

But the Kingdom is at your centre
and is about you.
When you know yourselves
then you will be known,
and you will be aware that you are
the sons of the Living Father.

Here the Father is also linked to the Kingdom—we are more familiar with that very Hebraic idea.

This linkage of the two ways of speaking also appears in logion 61, where Salome speaks (unexpectedly) in the Greek idiom 'Is it even as he from the One that . . .', and he replies in the Hebraic –

I am he who is,
from Him who is the same;
what was my Father's has been given to me.

Later, as Jesus asserts his nature there is logion 77 –

I am the light that is above them all.
I am the All.
The All comes forth from me,
and the All reaches towards me.
Cleave the wood, I am there;
lift up the stone,
and you shall find me there.

This is not a way of saying, as the Greeks might have done, that he is a spirit inhabiting the wood and the stone, but is to help us to see that it is the ultimate quality within us that gives the awareness of material and spiritual things, to enable all of these to become a Oneness.

There are two logia in which this Gospel helps us to recognize that whenever in the spiritual a duality, a pair, is noted, with further seeking an underlying unity or overriding oneness is to be found. To many this truism may be first experienced when a man and woman wed, and find the oneness of marriage –

. . . for many who are first shall become last
and they shall be a single One. (*Logion 4*)

. . . For in the place where the beginning is,
there shall be the end. (*Logion 18*)

In the first the seeker will find the Place of Life and will live; in the second he will find the happiness of a life independent of death.

We are given a parable about Oneness –
The Kingdom is like a shepherd
who owned a hundred sheep.
One among them, which was the largest, went astray;
he left the ninety-nine,
he sought after the one until he found it.
When he had toiled, he said to the sheep:
I desire you more than the ninety-nine!   (*Logion 107*)

The One was greater than the others, by seeking he found
it; it was a labour, the outcome of which he desired more
than all else.   It was the man in this state of realization that
is to be likened to the Kingdom.   The forms of the parable
with which we are familiar seem to have been simplified,
and the additions of a little one that went astray (*Matthew
18:12–14*) or of a sinner who repents (*Luke 15:3–7*) take
us away from the central point that the desire for Oneness
leads to the Kingdom.

The most significant step on the way to Oneness lies in
the recognition of the ego and the real Self, and in the work
to overcome the dominance of that ego acting in the mind
so that the real Self reveals its full power.   Logion 67 gives
a warning about this –

He who would understand the All with his mind,
but if he lacks his true Self
he will be deprived of the All.

while logion 106 speaks positively –

When you each make the two One
you will all become Sons of man,
and if you say:
"Mountain move away,"
it shall move.

The grandest sweep appears in logion 22, showing so

many ways in which duality is to be overcome, and material elements replaced by spiritual. The disciples ask Jesus how they are to enter the Kingdom, to which he proclaims –

> When you make the two One,
> and you make the inner even as the outer,
> and the outer even as the inner,
> and the above even as the below,
> so that you make the male and the female
> into a single One,
> in order that the male is not made male
> nor the female made female;
> when you make an eye in place of the eyes,
> and a hand in place of a hand,
> and a foot in place of a foot,
> and an image in place of an image,
> then shall you enter the Kingdom.

To change your Knowing

The word *metanoia* occurs only once in the Gospel of Thomas. However for anyone who wishes to benefit from this Gospel it is not only the most important word but it is crucially important.

This is a Greek word; at the time that our manuscript was translated there was no Coptic equivalent, so it appears in Greek ΜΕΤΑΝΟΕΙ. Nor is there any word in our language to translate it, it is better to learn to use it as it is. It is a word that occurs frequently in the Bible, very often in the sayings of Jesus. Because of its importance—wherever it is used—many authors have written books about it. Dr Maurice Nicoll gives a specially valuable treatment in his *The Mark* [1]. He could combine his knowledge of psychology with a deep awareness of the inner meanings of spiritual teachings of both the West and the Near-East, giving him a wider perspective than could be obtained from Christianity alone. Thus he was exceptionally qualified to explain this word.

'The Greek particle *meta* is found in several words of comparatively ordinary usage, such as metaphor, metamorphosis. Let us take metaphor; it means transference of meaning. To speak metaphorically is to speak beyond the literal words, to carry over or beyond and so transfer the meaning of what is said beyond the words used. . . . Metamorphosis is used to describe the transformation of form in insect-life, the transformation of a grub into a butterfly—a transference or transformation of structure into entirely new structure, into something beyond. The particle *meta* therefore indicates transference, or transformation, or beyondness.

'The other part of this word—*noia*—is from the Greek word *nous*, which means mind. The word *metanoia* therefore has to do with transformation of the mind in its essential meaning.'

Maurice Nicholl wrote before the Gospel of Thomas had become available. As used in that, it is better to say *metanoia* means to change one's knowing. Although this probably was what Nicoll meant, to use this phrase makes it clear that this is not an action of the mind. It is a process carried out and perceived at a level that is beyond the mind. It is a change to that which is experienced at the very centre of one's being, when the word 'to know' has 'the meaning of a profound certainty known at the depth of one's being.' [2]

Another way of looking at it is as the consequence of establishing a new point of view, of looking at things with a new perspective. Thus the call of *metanoia* by Jesus is for 'a transformation of one's awareness, a change that comes about as a result of a new viewpoint.' [2]

Metanoia occurs in logion 28 –

Jesus said;
I stood up in the midst of the world
and I manifested to them in the flesh.
I found them all drunk;
I found none among them athirst,
and my soul was afflicted for the sons of men
because they are blind in their heart
and they do not see
that empty they came into the world
and that empty they seek to go out of the world again,
except that now they are drunk.
When they shake off their wine,
then they will change their knowing.

We were born empty of the ego, and seek to find that state again. But the luggage we accumulate on the journey blinds and drugs us. To hear the call to metanoia involves shaking that off.

The idea of this change at a fundamental level is also in logion 2 –

> Jesus said;
> Let him who seeks not cease from seeking
> until he finds;
> and when he finds, he will be disturbed;
> and when he is disturbed, he will marvel,
> and he shall reign over the All.

Here the word 'disturbed' carries the meaning of being stirred around, which is only little different from one's viewpoint being turned around. Certainly such a turning might leave one disturbed, but at the same time it leaves one marvelling. The acceptance of anything new from Jesus can only leave one marvelling at the wonder, power and life-giving force of the revelation.

The tragedy—for us, no lesser word can be used—is that *metanoia* is almost always translated in the Bible as 'to repent' or with its noun 'repentance'. Nicoll again: "The English word repentance is derived from the Latin *poenitare* which means 'to feel sorry'. Penitence, feeling sorry, feeling pain or regret—this is a mood experienced by everyone from time to time. But the Greek word *metanoia* stands far above such a meaning . . ." [1] This comes about because when the Bible, originally written in Greek, was translated into the Latin Vulgate *poenitare* was used. Whenever it occurs, one should look at what it is that one is to feel penitence about. It is always for one's sins. It would be not too difficult to guess that this translation occurred, and is maintained today even though every modern translator knows about this, because it was influenced by, and supports, the doctrine introduced by Paul into the established Church of our sinfulness and the need to accept redemption from Christ.   And if one looks at the Gospels of the Bible there are only very few occasions when Jesus speaks of sin;   most of these, in the canonical version, are when he has released a person from some dread physical or mental illness—and to imply that He spoke thus to a sufferer cannot be made to harmonize with the idea of the compassionate Son of the Loving Father.

Therefore, instead of Jesus leading us into a new life, of urging us to change our Knowing, he is made to say that he is calling us to be penitent and to feel contrition.   An implication is given, or even expressed explicitly, that he is referring to our sins.   In the Gospel of Thomas a bad man may bring forth ill from the wicked storehouse of his heart *(logion 45)*.   The rest of us may be called impoverished, or blind, or drunk, or lacking, or divided, or generally missing the mark. [1]   Any of these is to be countered by coming to know ourselves or seeking after the treasure, by seeing, by shaking off the wine, by understanding the All, by being emptied of the ego, [3]   or generally trying again with better aim.

Those are all different, in a very fundamental way, from being evil, for which penitence is required.

The Church that treasured the Gospel of Thomas used this and also the Gospel of Matthew, perhaps in an earlier form than we have it now.   It is most illuminating to read that Gospel and whenever the words 'to repent' or 'repentance' occur to change them mentally into 'to change one's inner knowing', or to see a call to look at things from a new viewpoint.   A real transformation !

---

[1]   Published posthumously by Robinson & Watkins, London, 1954, and republished by Element Books, 1990;   especially the section on pages 87 to 112, although it occurs throughout the book.

[2]   Note for logion 28 in the *Presentation*.

[3]   Logia 3 and 76, 28, 67, 61 respectively.

154

Images

There are four logia in the Gospel of Thomas that refer to images –

> . . . when you make . . .
> an image in place of an image,
> then shall you enter the Kingdom.   (*part of logion 22*)

> We came from the light
> there, where the light was, by itself.
> It stood up and it manifested in their image.   (*Logion 50*)

> The images are manifest to man
> and the light that is amongst them is hidden.
> In the image of the light of the Father
> the light will reveal itself
> and his image is hidden by his light.   (*Logion 83*)

> In the days you see your resemblance, you rejoice.
> But when you see your images
> that in the beginning were in you,
> which neither die nor are manifest,
> oh! how will you bear the revelation !   (*Logion 84*)

This essay is an exploration of the different levels of meaning of 'images'. The Greek word ΕΙΚωΝ is used in our Gospel (even though with a slightly variant Coptic spelling), from which of course we get ikon today. An image may be thought of as being like a casting derived from a pattern; it is an exact replica, not the original.

The first quotation is the culmination of a long series of phrases, each one contrasting a spiritual form with a mental or material form. It is telling us to find the spiritual meaning of 'ikon'. An ikon is not a representation. Michelangelo gave us on the ceiling of the Sistine Chapel the greatest visual representation of God, to convey symbolically by the touch of fingers the passing of divine quality into man. An ikon of the Eastern Orthodox Church is different. It is an exact copy, but not the original, of a form invested with spiritual significance. The artist who paints each particular ikon serves a long training under a master, and makes a copy that retains all the details of the original, thereby conveying the symbolism unsullied.

So in the first logion we are to find a spiritual form of something that previously may have been a mental idea; to rise to the spiritual level above a mere thought-form. It is one of the gateways into the Kingdom.

In the second logion the first two phrases speak of our coming from the self-existing light; we saw this in the baby, and hence in ourselves. But in the third phrase we are suddenly taken to a very much higher level. The light was manifested in *their* image. 'Their' relates to 'we', these are the only plural words in the logion. So, however startling it may seem, we are being told the light is the image of us. The original is the highest in mankind, the light is its replica.

Logion 83 starts with the mental images we make but, because they come from the ego—of which the ordinary mind is a part—the light within them is hidden. However, the light of the Father is the true light and, as we find that, the true light reveals itself. So far, so good. However, we need to look at the third phrase more closely. It is not saying the image of the Father, such as in the idea we might have of 'man being made in the image of God'. It is the first part of a longer expression that spans over three phrases. In the last of those 'his image is hidden' is a way of saying the Father is imageless,

he is the original.   And so his imageless nature is hidden by
his light.   This is the same as where we can say 'the light
reveals', and 'the brilliance of the light conceals'.   Yet we have
also been told that the light is the image of man.   So this is a
paradox of the conjunction of opposites, for the grasping of
which it is necesary to get beyond the words and the mind—
to get into the experience of Oneness which usually can only
be found in contemplation.   Here we have an instance of a
description of the indescribable, a definition of the indefinable,
an expression of the inexpressible.   This is a *via media*
attempting to convey something that cannot be expressed in
language, but only experienced.

Logion 84 is a complement to the preceding one.   In its first
phrase it reminds us of the rejoicing we feel as we recognize
that what is at our centre resembles the light.   Then, going
on, we come to see that this image was pre-existent, it does not
need to manifest itself because it was always there, and it is not
affected by our death (essay *Death and resurrection*).   Put
another way, the image of the light within us is eternal, not in
the sense that it goes on for ever but in the much more
profound sense that it is independent of time.   It is just in this
way that by finding the inner meaning of the logia it is said a
man will not taste death (*logia 1 and 19*).   By finding the inner
meaning of these logia he will find Life that is independent of
death.   This, indeed, can be a revelation that is almost
overwhelming. ★

There will be some who recognize in all this a similarity to
the teachings of Socrates as recorded by Plato, and especially
to the thought and writings of Plotinus ★ who in the middle of
the third century combined those with the teachings of

★ Literally, the final phrase is 'How much will you bear!', it being characteristic
that the key word is left unwritten; the insight into the rendering as it is
presented was given to the author by Professor Quispel.

★ W R Inge, *The Philosophy of Plotinus*, 1928, Longmans.

Christianity. He must surely have known the Gospel of Thomas, for his city of Alexandria then had the finest library in the world. Some of the words will be different, for they used expressions such as 'forms' or the 'philosophy of ideas'. There are others so deeply knowledgible in these that they may be inclined to think that they were the source for these sayings. That is to say, that someone took those Platonic or Neoplatonic ideas and put them into the mouth of Jesus.

This sort of approach overlooks an important possibility. We know that while still a boy Jesus stayed behind from his family to sit with the rabbis and priests in the Temple to question and learn from them. Here is the evidence for an intense seeking and questing for spiritual Truth. Who are we to imply that this did not continue throughout the next fifteen years? Surely he must have sought out every source of spiritual enlightenment—the Essenes, the Gnostics and the Greeks. Admittedly the general Hellinistic environment in which he lived was only a poor rustic shadow of the glory of Greek civilization. But the real thing flourished in Alexandria, and there was constant travel between his country and the great city states of Greece.

Not only that. Palestine was at or near the trading routes between India and the West. In that country there was an awareness of spiritual Truth that by then had been fully developed for at least two millenia. It had long before been set down in their scriptures, and was enshrined in great souls who had realized this Truth. They could readily travel, either overland or by boats along the coasts, with the traders. Their speech would be known in the markets. Symbolic may it be, but we would be very unhappy to dismiss Luke's account of three wise men coming from the east to honour the birth of Jesus. In our day there are such seers, who either seek out the infant to be the heir presumptive Dalai Lama, or seek out one who is worthy and open to receive their very special gifts.

Their ability to see is independent of space or distance. Who are we to imply that those could not see Jesus in his young manhood, and did not come to give to him treasures from their long spiritual tradition?

Today, in the jumbo-jets thousands * travel daily from the West to and from India; others go on to the Far East with its Zen tradition. A proportion (admittedly only a tiny one) of these also seek out those spiritual teachings. They too will find echos, expressed in different words, with much in the Gospel of Thomas. The plain fact is that our recognition that there is only a single spiritual Truth must keep pace with this creation of a single world brought about by our technological achievements.

Our troubles and limitations in the West arose from the exclusivity inherent in the claim that Jesus was the *only* Son of God, coupled with the blinkered view that he realized and culminated the Hebrew tradition. One of the great values of the Gospel of Thomas is to show that Jesus, through his recorded words, was an exemplar of the unity of all Truth.

---

*   Just study the airline timetables: at least 2000 people daily, every day of the year.

Sin and suffering

There are only two mentions of sin in the Gospel of Thomas. They each take a rather peculiar form. The first in logion 14 –

Jesus said to them:
If you fast you will beget a sin to yourselves,
and if you pray you will be condemned,
and if you give alms
you will do harm to your spirits. . . .

and in the second, logion 104, when after the disciples have mentioned praying and fasting Jesus says –

What therefore is the sin that I have committed
or in what have I been overcome?

While each goes on to give a positive approach, what may be noted here is that only little emphasis is placed on the word. However, what is more significant is to recognize that sin is elsewhere always associated with judgement. One of the most noticeable differences between the Gospel of Thomas and the Gospels of the Bible as they have come down to us is that it is free from judgement; the word condemnation occurs only in the quotation above. Certainly, as recorded by Thomas, Jesus went around without judging, threatening or condemning people. It was a teaching from which fear was absent.

Unless one has done it already, it may come as something of a surprise to find that in the Gospels of the Bible Jesus also seldom speaks of sin—even then mostly in John's, rarely in the

others. When he does it is usually linking up with the
thinking of his hearers, for sin looms large in the Old
Testament. Furthermore, those who are keen on the origin
of words explain that 'to sin' comes from the idea of missing
the mark. However Ronald Blackburn writes wisely in a
Quaker journal * –

> 'In his healing ministry Jesus often recognized a
> sufferer's illness to be associated with a sense of guilt;
> hence the need for forgiveness. By his word of
> forgiveness it may be said that Jesus removed the guilt,
> or 'took away the sins' which had brought suffering
> to those who came to him in their distress. Jesus was
> once accused by his religious critics of receiving and
> consorting with sinners. These were not necessarily
> moral sinners but religious outcasts, shunned by the
> good churchmen of the day for in their daily conduct
> they had habitually failed to observe the requirements
> of established religion. This ministry of forgiveness by
> Jesus may be best understood as one whereby all who
> had been rejected now found themselves freely accepted
> by Jesus. The genuine sinners in particular discovered
> that their personal failures did not stand in the way
> of their being received in friendship. . . . It is
> remarkable how rarely, if ever, Jesus used the words
> 'sin' or 'sinner' in any condemnatory sense when
> brought face to face with individuals with their personal
> moral failures and delinquencies.'

Evil, the bedfellow of sin, certainly abounds in our world,
whether in the wickedness of nations, organizations or
individuals. One logion only in the Gospel of Thomas refers
to it –

---

* *Salvation in the New Testament Experience*, Friends' Quarterly, vol. 25,
October 1989, somewhat shortened.

A good man brings forth good out of his storehouse,
a bad man brings forth ill
out of his wicked storehouse
which is in his heart,
and he speaks ill:
for out of the abundance of the heart
he brings forth ill.   (*Logion 45*)

As so often we are being told that the preceding sentence
should have been written 'individuals, organizations and
nations'—wickedness comes from people. And it goes on to
emphasize that it comes from the heart. The Gospel of
Thomas goes no further to tell us from whence it comes, it
leaves us to work that out for ourselves. So what might be its
source?

As we look at instances of evil, rather than attributing them
to some external power or influence—for which there is no
evidence in the words of Jesus either in the Biblical Gospels
or this one—we will be driven to identify their source in
such emotions as fear, avarice, greed, covetousness, lust,
domination, the quest for power, destructiveness, viciousness,
immorality. These may all be seen as negative or dark
emotions. Most certainly in this teaching such emotions stem
from the ego, therein lies the source of evil—and hence their
power.

As for suffering, there is no specific mention of it in the
Gospel of Thomas. Since this is perhaps mankind's greatest
burden this may seem to be most inexplicable. All the more
so since the Gospels of the Bible give many instances of
suffering—whether of the body or the mind or the psyche—
and of people being released from it by Jesus. And all through
the centuries one of the greatest solaces to many has been the
awareness that Jesus shared in an extreme form the kinds of
suffering that may befall us. For this reason, if not any other,

the omission from this Gospel of all mention of his passion may appear as an ultimate weakness.

Here we are faced again with the absence in the Gospel of Thomas, and in all the other books that survive of the early Church based upon it, of emphasis on the crucifixion of Jesus. We have already seen (essay *Death and resurrection*) that man's burden of the fear of death, and the distress of the bereaved, is here not answered by a doctrine of an afterlife which, subject to judgement, may be in paradise or hell. Rather, he is encouraged to become aware of the culmination of a Life in the here and now that is independent of death.

Likewise, there is the possibility that this Gospel is recording a teaching that is intended to make us search for a release from the burden, which may be even greater, of suffering. We have seen that one of the most crucial elements in this Gospel, the coming to be aware of the nature and significance of one's ego, is not mentioned specifically—it is hidden in the sense of being something to be searched for so that, when found, its knowing may be all the more vivid. This may well be the clue to follow.

Suffering may befall us in the body, with excruciating pain that must have been even harder to bear in his day than in ours thanks to our doctors. It may befall us in the mind, as we inwardly toss and turn in perplexities. It may befall us in our emotions, giving distress, anguish, depression or despair. It may befall some of us as an illness or distortion of our minds or emotions, to become enfeebled or confused. But where do these calamitous effects have their place, from whence do they derive their power? It must be in the ego, for they cannot exist in the Self. To dim the power of the ego may be the route to the overcoming of suffering. Sometimes we can see this, in a person who in any ordinary terms would seem to be deeply suffering, but whose light in the soul shines brightly—it can even be a revelation to witness.

Thus suffering may bring about the reduction of the ego. And suffering is involved in being rid of the dominance of the ego, it is often likened to a cleansing fire. ★ It may be seen that symbolically Jesus spent forty days in the desert to extinguish the last trace of ego of his humanity, to fit him for the start of his mission. But in us it is the ego that is suffering. Suffering belongs to the ego; the ego is suffering for its own demise. Following that further, it may be possible to answer the mystery of why one, himself egoless and totally given to helping others, chose a particular way to make the ultimate gift to mankind.

In this Gospel as the ego is brought under the real Self, dimmed until only One remains, however high the mountain of distress and suffering may appear to be, we are promised –

> If two make peace with each other
> in this single house,
> they will say to the mountain
> "Move away"
> and it shall move.   *(Logion 48)*

It is conspicuous that of sin, evil and suffering the Gospel of Thomas is giving only clues to the way forward. So let us turn in the next essay to a theme that shines bright and clear.

★ For example, Irma Tweedie, *The Chasm of Fire*, 1979, Element Books.

The Beatitudes and Happiness

ΜΑΚΑριος, a Greek word pronounced makarios, is used ten times in the Gospel of Thomas. The only key-words used more frequently are the Kingdom, to find, to know, the living and the light. It is used as a noun; it would be rather wonderful if we could say in our language 'a happy'. In accepted translation it may be rendered either as happy or blessed; for the *Presentation* happy has been chosen because happiness comes essentially from within, whereas being blessed is associated with a giver.

In the Gospels of Matthew and Luke which include many beatitudes it is merely a literary convention that they are mainly grouped together, just as John has presented many of Jesus' greatest teachings as the farewell discourses at the Last Supper. It is apparent that the sayings of Jesus with ΜΑΚΑΡΙΟς must have been given on many different occasions, as prompted by the opportunity or situation. Can we allow ourselves to visualize Jesus going about with his disciples—which the chauvinistic assumptions of the evangelists limited to the twelve with hardly any mention of the women who must have also been present—carrying an aura about him that led to the frequent use of this word?

Even so, happiness and to be happy in English may not immediately carry the intended meaning. It is not so much merriment as joy or bliss, associated with a profound contentment. It does not appear so much as laughter (although it may come as a great challenge to us to visualize Jesus laughing with his disciples) but as a poise and radiance.

It is derived not from a response to external events (quite different from being happy with a new car or a well-baked cake coming out of the oven) but from a condition or state of being within. It may be regarded as a flowering of the Self, so that any of the sayings 'Happy is he who does so-and-so' is a pointer towards coming to an awareness of what lies within.

Of the ten beatitudes in Thomas only two closely correspond to those in the Bible –

> Happy are the poor,
> for yours is the Kingdom of the heavens.
> > *(Logion 54, Matthew 5:3, Luke 6:20)*

> . . . Happy are they who are hungry,
> so that the belly of him who desires
> shall be satisfied.
> > *(Logion 69, Matthew 5:6. Luke 6:21)*

To which may be added logion 90 *(Matthew 11:28)* –

> Jesus said:
> Come to me,
> for easy is my yoke
> and my lordship is gentle,
> and you shall find repose for yourselves.

Logia 7, 18, 19, 49, 58, 68 and 103 also all use ΜΑΚΑρΙΟς. A few of these have parallels (see *Annex* to essay *Comparisons with the Bible*) while most are unique to Thomas. All of them have been used in one or another of this set of essays, but in the present context it may be well to be reminded of two –

> Happy are the 'loners' and the chosen
> for you shall find the Kingdom.
> Because you are from the heart of it,
> you shall go there again.   *(Logion 49)*

Happy is the man who has toiled to lose the ego,
he has found the Life.   (*Logion 58*)

Form a picture in the inner eye of Jesus striding about or sitting with his disciples around him, and their joyousness of being in his presence. Almost certainly this will be done as one is a loner, but perhaps it is easiest when amidst a group known as friends whom we trust and know will always support us. Hear him calling "Metanoia, follow me" and feel him working to change your knowing, to discern the old luggage and have courage to throw it overboard. Listen as he speaks so often of the Kingdom, the All, the Oneness to which he is taking people. This is a journey of finding, where something new is found, and leads to a Place that is known deep within.

Seek for the inner meaning that is hidden in the words we have been given but lies beyond them. Work will be needed to find these treasures; as this effort includes struggles with the ego there will arise great turbulent disturbances. With the example of his egolessness, find guidance and support. As the ego is weakened, as its veil is drawn back, that light that is latent within may respond to the radiance he presents. This living quality is highly infectious, so that he becomes the Life-Giver. It becomes a movement with a repose, an assurance, a tranquillity, a peace, happiness itself.

Index to Logia

Key: 'a' means all; 'p' means part; 'r' means reference only

Key: 'a' means all; 'p' means part; 'r' means reference only

Key: 'a' means all;   'p' means part;   'r' means reference only